United States
Department of
Agriculture

Forest Service

Southern
Research Station

Resource Bulletin
SRS–139

Trends in Southern Pulpwood Production, 1953–2006

Tony G. Johnson,
Carolyn D. Steppleton,
and Michael Howell

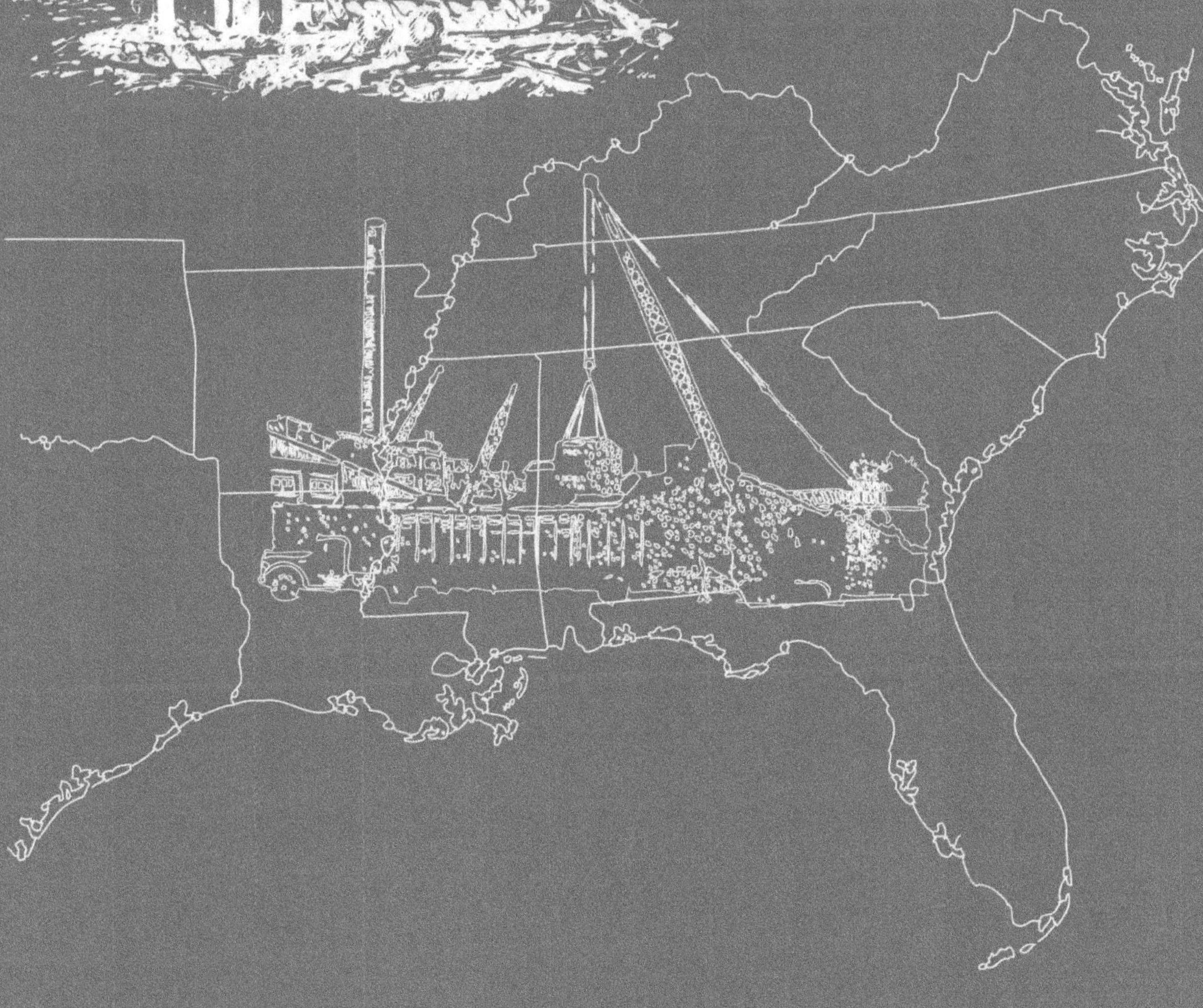

I0410883

September 2008

Southern Research Station
200 W.T. Weaver Blvd.
Asheville, NC 28804

Trends in Southern Pulpwood Production, 1953–2006

Tony G. Johnson, Forester
Forest Inventory and Analysis,
Forest Service, Southern Research Station
U.S. Department of Agriculture, Knoxville, TN,

Carolyn D. Steppleton, Statistical Assistant
Forest Inventory and Analysis,
Forest Service, Southern Research Station
U.S. Department of Agriculture, Asheville, NC,

Michael Howell, Forester
Forest Inventory and Analysis,
Forest Service, Southern Research Station
U.S. Department of Agriculture, Knoxville, TN

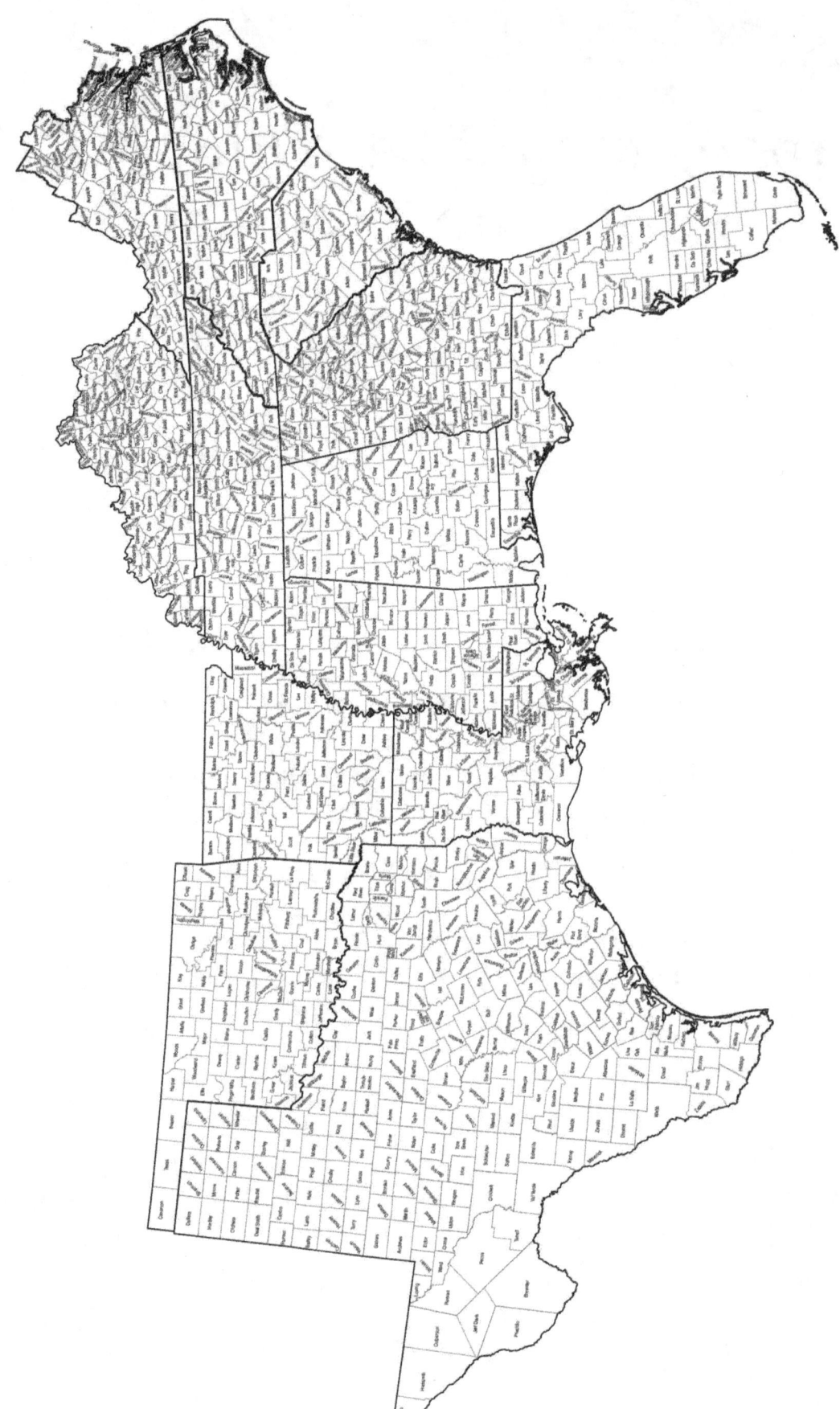

Figure 1—The 13 Southern States and the counties and parishes of each.

Introduction

This publication contains historical pulpwood production data derived from canvasses of wood-using pulpmills that have drawn roundwood or wood residues from lands within the 13 Southern States (fig. 1). The canvasses of southern pulpmills have been conducted annually for more than 60 years. Between 1949 and 1993 the Southern and the Southeastern Forest Experiment Stations of the Forest Service, U.S. Department of Agriculture, alternatively compiled, analyzed, and reported the pulpwood canvass. In 1995 the two units were combined to form the Southern Research Station; and 1 year earlier the Commonwealth of Kentucky had been added to comprise the total, contiguous area from which data are routinely gathered and disseminated in a variety of inventory and analysis reports. Kentucky's pulpwood production data from 1962 to the present are included in this report. Annual pulpmill canvasses were conducted to determine the amount and source of pulpwood receipts by county and to determine interstate and cross-regional movement of industrial roundwood. County level and cross-regional movement of roundwood is not addressed in this report, because such data are voluminous, considering the number of years covered.

Pulpwood production data are combined with other data that are provided by the periodic canvasses of all primary wood-using plants conducted in the Southern States. Such combinations provide a nearly complete picture of total industrial timber product output. These data are used to augment the Forest Inventory and Analysis annual inventory of timber removals; i.e., they provide product proportions of (total) removals, which are used to quantify products from each State's timberland. Production volumes in this bulletin are reported in standard cords (5,400 and 5,600 pounds per cord for softwood and hardwood, respectively), green tons, and thousand cubic feet.

Pulpwood

Pulpwood production, like many other commodities production, varies with the ups and downs of the Nation's economy. Relatively stable economic conditions that prevailed over the last one-half of the 20th century created a nearly constant increased demand for pulpwood. The rise in population, combined with an increase in the per capita consumption of paper, paperboard, and other nonpaper products of pulpwood, helped bring an expansion throughout the industry and fueled the general upward trend in pulpwood production through the late 1990s. In the 2005 RPA Timber Assessment Update, Haynes reported that from the late 1990s to 2002 the strength in the U.S. dollar—compared to other world currencies in the period—offset U.S. industrial competitiveness and contributed to an overall decline in industrial production during that period (Haynes and

others 2007). Southern pulpwood production peaked in 1997 at 75.9 million cords, or nearly 201 million green tons. However, global competition, coupled with more stringent environmental standards, a leveling demand for paper products, and an aging infrastructure, had taken its toll on the industry and overall production. In addition, the number of pulpmills in the South has declined over the last several years. Notwithstanding this downturn, however, southern pulpwood production increased nearly fourfold from 16.2 million cords (43.9 million green tons) in 1953 to 64.7 million cords (170.9 million green tons) in 2006 (table A.1a). Total pulpwood production on southern timberlands over the last 53 years has totaled more than 2.6 billion cords (7.0 billion green tons). This volume constitutes nearly 253 million truckloads of wood. If the total cords harvested were stacked end to end, the resulting 4.0 million miles of wood could circle the earth 161 times or go to the moon and return 8 times. Tables A.2a–A.2c and A.3a–A.3c display total production volumes by year for the Southeastern region (Florida, Georgia, North Carolina, South Carolina, and Virginia) and the South Central region (Alabama, Arkansas, Kentucky, Louisiana, Mississippi, Oklahoma, Tennessee, and Texas). Table A.4 displays the total number of southern pulpmills and capacity by year, while tables A.5a through A.17c display total production volumes by year for each of the Southern States.

Roundwood

Several significant trends in the southern pulpwood industry have taken place over the last five decades. In the early 1950s combined softwood and hardwood roundwood pulpwood production amounted to 1.0 billion cubic feet, or about 25 percent of total industrial product output for the South and 57 percent of the Nation's total pulpwood production (U.S. Department of Agriculture 1958). By 1970, pulpwood production as a proportion of total industrial product output had reached 48 percent, or more than 2.5 billion cubic feet. This proportion remained relatively stable until the late 1990s when pulpwood production as a proportion of total product output began to decline. In 2005, at 3.4 billion cubic feet, pulpwood accounted for 40 percent of the South's total industrial roundwood output and 75 percent of the Nation's total pulpwood production (Johnson and others 2008; Smith and others 2008, in press). Softwood roundwood production has more than doubled—from 14.1 million cords (38.2 million green tons) in 1953 to 31.7 million cords (85.7 million green tons) in 2006. However, softwood roundwood expressed as a percent of total production declined significantly until the mid-1980s (fig. 2). In 1953, softwood roundwood supplied 87 percent of the total pulpwood production. By 1986, it made up only 45 percent of total production and

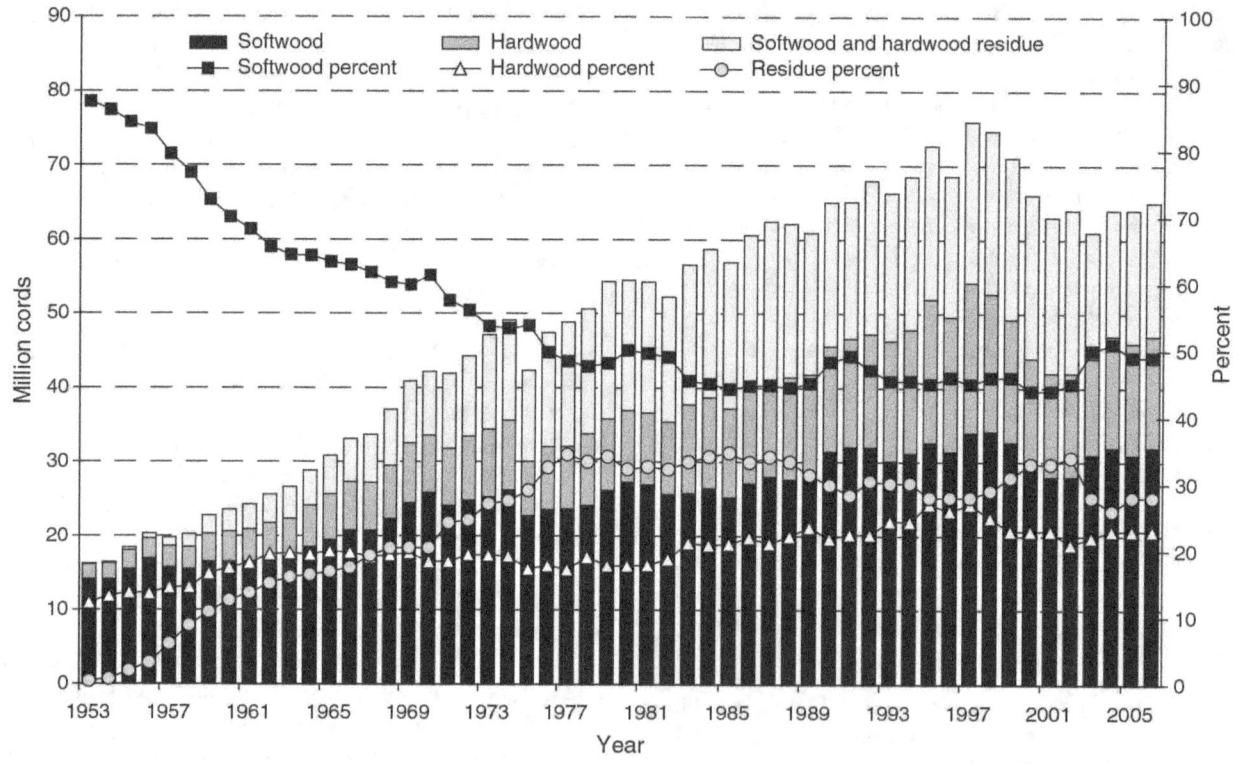

Figure 2—Pulpwood production in the South, 1953–2006.

remained relatively stable until 2002. Softwood roundwood production has increased over the last few years and now accounts for about one-half of total pulpwood production. The decline in softwood roundwood as a percent of total wood used was offset by the trend toward greater utilization of wood (mill) residues and the abundant hardwood resources in the South.

Production methods and techniques developed over the last 50 years have enabled the pulp industry to use greater quantities of hardwood. Hardwood roundwood production has climbed from slightly <2.0 million cords (5.5 million green tons) in 1953 to more than 14.6 million cords (40.9 million green tons) in 2006. In 1953, hardwood roundwood furnished only 12 percent of total production and peaked in 1997 at 27 percent, or more than 20 million cords. However, since 1997 hardwood roundwood production has declined, and in 2006 it accounted for 23 percent of total production.

Wood Residues

Mills reported two types of receipts: (1) roundwood and (2) wood residues. Wood residues primarily are mill residue chips, a byproduct of sawmilling and veneer mill operations.

Chips produced in the woods or when material received as roundwood by primary producers is chipped instead of being milled are not technically mill residues, but are reported as such in this and other resource bulletins. Figure 2 illustrates the dramatic increase in the utilization of wood residues for pulpwood. In 1953, the proportion of wood residues used for pulpwood was almost negligible at <1 percent. Wood residues used to make pulpwood increased from nearly 76,000 cords (185,000 green tons) in 1953 to more than 18.3 million cords (44.4 million green tons) in 2006. Wood residue as a proportion of total use has remained relatively stable since the late 1970s, peaked at 35 percent in 1985, and accounted for 28 percent of total pulpwood production in 2006.

Mills and Pulping Capacity

In 1953, 61 southern pulpmills were operating and drawing wood from the 13 Southern States (table A.4). Mill construction proceeded at a feverish pace during the mid- and late 1950s and again during the late 1960s and early 1970s. During the 20-year period between 1953 and 1973, 52 new mills were constructed, more than tripling daily pulping capacity. The total number of pulpmills drawing wood from the South peaked at 129 in 1979, 117 of those mills were operating in Southern States and 12 were in surrounding States. Even though the number of mills declined to 87 in 2006, the average daily pulping capacity increased steadily through expansion and modernization of existing facilities (fig. 3). In 1953, the combined daily pulping capacity of southern mills was 28,670 tons, or an average of 470 tons per mill, and accounted for about one-half of the Nation's total pulping capacity (Cruikshank 1954). Southern pulping capacity steadily increased and accounted for 60 percent of the Nation's pulping capacity by 1961 and reached 70 percent by 1974 (Smith and others 2003). Daily pulping capacity in the South peaked in 1998 at 140,610 tons per day. In 2006, the 87 southern pulpmills had a combined daily pulping capacity of 125,093 tons per day and averaged 1,438 tons per mill, still accounting for more than 70 percent of the Nation's total pulping capacity (fig. 2) (Johnson and Steppleton 2008). Mills operating outside southern borders but drawing some of their wood from the South have fluctuated between 2 and 14 mills over the last five decades.

Outlook

Over the last 53 years, pressures on pulpwood suppliers to reduce costs and increase production have substantially improved harvesting techniques. The traditional short-stick pulpwood harvest operations of the early 1950s have been completely replaced by totally mechanized tree-length harvesting operations. Mechanical tree harvesters and in-woods chipping operations have allowed almost total tree utilization in softwoods and very high utilization rates in hardwoods as well. Recent harvest and utilization studies conducted in Georgia and Alabama indicate that nearly one-half of the softwood volume being harvested for pulpwood in those States is coming from pine plantations (Bentley and Harper 2007). This percentage will no doubt go even higher in the next few years due to the maturation of the Conservation Reserve Program pine plantations established in the mid-1980s and early 1990s. Utilization of wood residues from primary processors is equally high. The 2005 timber products assessment for the South showed wood

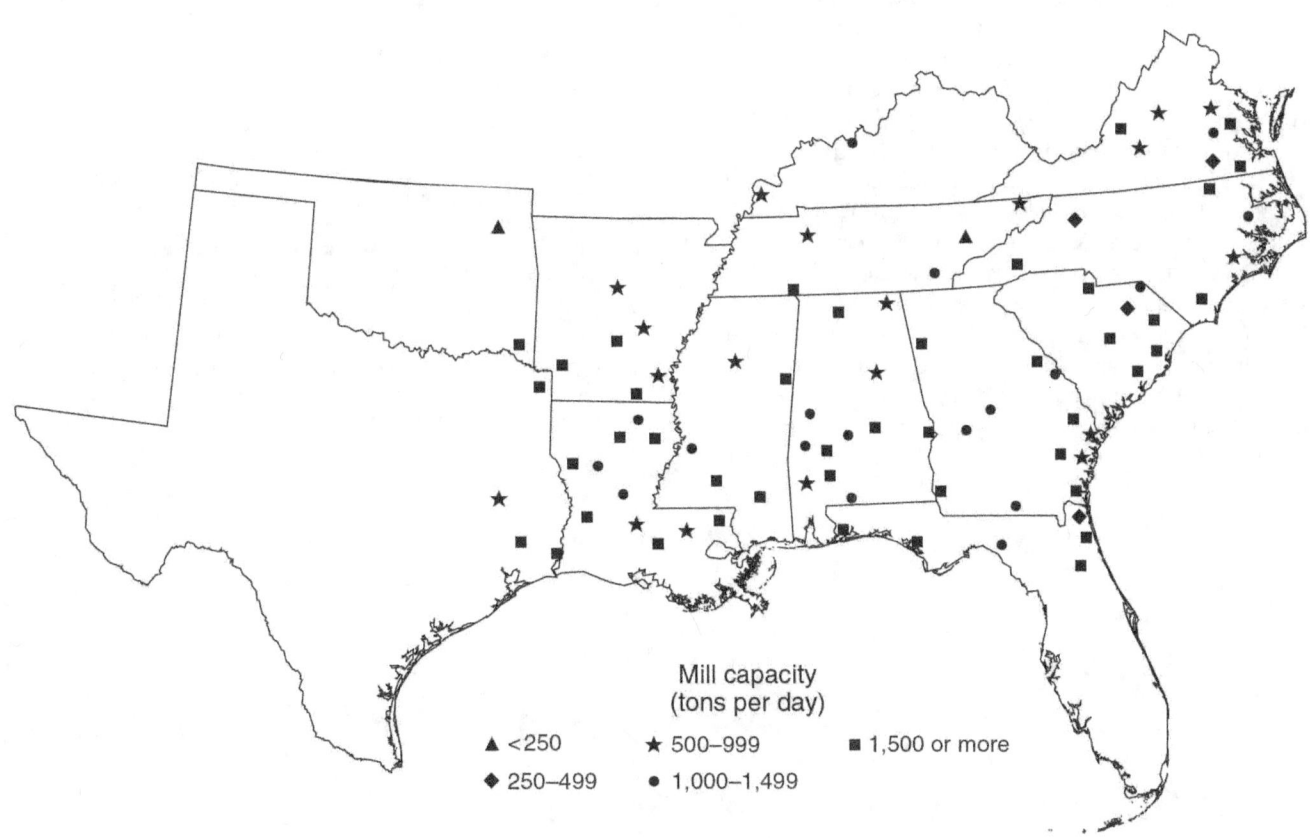

Figure 3—2005 capacity of southern pulpmills operating and drawing wood from the 13 Southern States.

3

residue use at almost 100 percent (Johnson and others 2008). Of the 1.3 billion cubic feet of coarse residue produced mostly by southern sawmills and veneer mills in 2005 more than 1.0 billion cubic feet, or 82 percent, was sent to pulpmills for fiber production.

According to the 2005 RPA Timber Assessment Update tonnage of U.S. paper and paperboard consumption increased at an annual average rate of 2.8 percent between 1960 and the peak in 1999. A weaker dollar since 2002 has contributed to a gradual rebound in industrial production, but structural changes in demand have led to a slower projected growth. Between 2005 and 2050 the 2005 update projection envisions an average growth rate of just 0.7 percent for the period. U.S. per capita consumption of paper and paperboard is projected to remain relatively flat at the current level of 700 pounds per capita (Haynes and others 2007). As reported earlier in this report, technical innovations over the last 50 years have led to increased use of hardwoods, mill residues, as well as an increased use of recycled waste paper since the mid-1980s. In fact, wastepaper recovery was projected to reach 52 percent for 2006.

Thanks to the determination and perseverance of paper scientists on both the supplier and production sides of the industry, U.S. paper companies are rapidly closing in on the goal of 55 percent wastepaper recovery rates by 2012 (PaperAge 2006). Haynes and others (2007) reported that the increased paper recycling rates have had a pronounced impact on growth in softwood pulpwood receipts at wood pulpmills from the mid-1980s to 1990s. Softwood pulpwood receipts are projected to increase at an average annual growth rate of 0.9 percent per year between 2005 and 2050, while hardwood pulpwood receipts are projected to increase by only 0.4 percent per year for the same period. By virtue of its tremendous pulping capacity, the South is projected to remain the dominant U.S. region in production of wood fiber products and in pulpwood supply and demand (Ince and Durbak 2002).

Literature Cited

Bentley, James W.; Harper, Richard A. 2007. Georgia's harvest and utilization study, 2004. Resour. Bull. SRS–117. Asheville, NC: U.S. Department of Agriculture Forest Service, Southern Research Station. 25 p.

Cruikshank, James W. 1954. 1953 pulpwood production in the South. For. Surv. Release 43. Asheville, NC: U.S. Department of Agriculture Forest Service, Southeastern Forest Experiment Station. 32 p.

Haynes, Richard W.; Adams, Darius M.; Alig, Ralph J. [and others]. 2007. The 2005 RPA timber assessment update. Gen. Tech. Rep. PNW–GTR–699. Portland, OR: U.S. Department of Agriculture Forest Service, Pacific Northwest Research Station. 212 p.

Ince, Peter R.; Durbak, Irene. 2002. Pulpwood supply and demand—development in the South, little growth elsewhere. Journal of Forestry. 100(2): 20–25.

Johnson, Tony G.; Bentley, James W.; Howell, Michael. 2008. The South's timber industry—an assessment of timber product output and use, 2005. Resour. Bull. SRS–135. Asheville, NC: U.S. Department of Agriculture Forest Service, Southern Research Station. 52 p.

Johnson, Tony G.; Steppleton, Carolyn D. 2008. Southern pulpwood production, 2006. Resour. Bull. SRS–134. Asheville, NC: U.S. Department of Agriculture Forest Service, Southern Research Station. 32 p.

PaperAge. 2006. Stickies still a critical concern for today's recycling plants. http://www.paperage.com/issue_archives.html. [Date accessed: April 2008].

Smith, Brad W.; Miles, Patrick D.; Perry, Charles H.; Pugh, Scott A. [In press]. Forest resources of the United States, 2007. Gen. Tech. Rep. Washington, DC: U.S. Department of Agriculture Forest Service.

Smith, Brett R.; Rice, Robert W.; Ince, Peter J. 2003. Pulp capacity in the United States, 2000. Gen. Tech. Rep. FPL–GTR–139. Madison, WI: U.S. Department of Agriculture Forest Service, Forest Products Laboratory. 23 p.

U.S. Department of Agriculture, Forest Service. 1958. Timber resources for America's future. For. Resour. Rep. 14. Washington, DC: U.S. Government Printing Office. 713 p.

Table A.1a—Pulpwood production in the South, by region and species group, 1953 to 2006

Year	Total southern production	Total Southeast	Total South Central	Roundwood Total	Roundwood Softwood	Roundwood Hardwood	Residues Total	Residues Softwood	Residues Hardwood
					standard cords				
1953	16,202,810	8,837,840	7,364,970	16,126,956	14,147,578	1,979,378	75,854	27,389	48,465
1954	16,395,805	8,884,130	7,511,675	16,269,642	14,107,964	2,161,678	126,163	85,758	40,405
1955	18,388,774	10,291,065	8,097,709	18,014,642	15,487,727	2,526,915	374,132	258,973	115,159
1956	20,344,875	11,272,250	9,072,625	19,685,736	16,920,042	2,765,694	659,139	503,171	155,968
1957	19,782,661	10,983,756	8,798,905	18,579,626	15,713,620	2,866,006	1,203,035	1,058,373	144,662
1958	20,232,753	11,021,489	9,211,264	18,447,363	15,502,786	2,944,577	1,785,390	1,588,924	196,466
1959	22,750,137	12,656,064	10,094,073	20,287,997	16,515,472	3,772,525	2,462,140	2,186,410	275,730
1960	23,551,036	13,303,645	10,247,391	20,595,515	16,490,979	4,104,536	2,955,521	2,583,663	371,858
1961	24,230,728	13,630,816	10,599,912	20,919,012	16,520,907	4,398,105	3,311,716	2,832,236	479,480
1962	25,668,494	14,380,875	11,287,619	21,813,989	16,800,896	5,013,093	3,854,505	3,227,194	627,311
1963	26,677,538	14,924,469	11,753,069	22,409,465	17,149,617	5,259,848	4,268,073	3,541,620	726,453
1964	28,918,765	15,972,302	12,946,463	24,193,093	18,555,980	5,637,113	4,725,672	3,946,437	779,235
1965	30,889,742	16,942,123	13,947,619	25,703,022	19,522,644	6,180,378	5,186,720	4,277,926	908,794
1966	33,216,094	17,560,369	15,655,725	27,427,129	20,818,663	6,608,466	5,788,965	4,628,822	1,160,143
1967	33,811,075	17,715,229	16,095,846	27,259,096	20,792,589	6,466,507	6,551,979	5,152,527	1,399,452
1968	37,252,488	18,588,225	18,664,263	29,583,616	22,348,602	7,235,014	7,668,872	6,145,000	1,523,872
1969	41,036,950	19,788,684	21,248,266	32,594,285	24,483,043	8,111,242	8,442,665	6,653,478	1,789,187
1970	42,392,072	20,517,428	21,874,644	33,662,584	25,847,530	7,815,054	8,729,488	6,574,306	2,155,182
1971	42,218,156	19,793,773	22,424,383	31,951,669	24,105,508	7,846,161	10,266,487	8,179,005	2,087,482
1972	44,599,642	20,745,072	23,854,570	33,555,170	24,829,538	8,725,632	11,044,472	8,886,214	2,158,258
1973	47,567,651	21,893,028	25,674,623	34,600,815	25,293,451	9,307,364	12,966,836	10,284,310	2,682,526
1974	49,498,544	22,485,394	27,013,150	35,749,215	26,215,317	9,533,898	13,749,329	10,403,228	3,346,101
1975	42,593,134	19,514,653	23,078,481	30,107,334	22,761,694	7,345,640	12,485,800	9,967,945	2,517,855
1976	47,674,460	21,778,823	25,895,637	32,079,343	23,592,363	8,486,980	15,595,117	12,600,753	2,994,364
1977	49,137,165	23,631,324	25,505,841	32,109,860	23,665,158	8,444,702	17,027,305	14,009,021	3,018,284
1978	50,907,026	24,154,458	26,752,568	33,816,812	24,117,644	9,699,168	17,090,214	13,850,281	3,239,933
1979	54,679,694	24,780,111	29,899,583	35,866,853	26,147,409	9,719,444	18,812,841	14,618,662	4,194,179
1980	54,874,621	24,805,820	30,068,801	37,054,234	27,283,428	9,770,806	17,820,387	13,484,531	4,335,856
1981	54,638,426	25,090,332	29,548,094	36,695,233	26,947,963	9,747,270	17,943,193	13,202,379	4,740,814
1982	52,599,162	24,615,865	27,983,297	35,516,377	25,623,977	9,892,400	17,082,785	13,005,481	4,077,304
1983	57,135,958	26,617,509	30,518,449	37,885,893	25,779,773	12,106,120	19,250,065	14,825,261	4,424,804
1984	59,257,644	27,569,807	31,687,837	38,832,834	26,466,982	12,365,852	20,424,810	15,430,351	4,994,459
1985	57,473,849	27,096,107	30,377,742	37,346,500	25,248,900	12,097,600	20,127,349	15,417,635	4,709,714
1986	60,970,329	28,132,108	32,838,221	40,608,411	27,140,721	13,467,690	20,361,918	15,570,518	4,791,400
1987	62,981,291	29,359,580	33,621,711	41,409,400	28,016,700	13,392,700	21,571,891	16,193,644	5,378,247
1988	62,683,834	28,698,590	33,985,244	41,656,100	27,663,200	13,992,900	21,027,734	15,590,921	5,436,813
1989	61,506,321	27,854,623	33,651,698	42,066,100	27,507,000	14,559,100	19,440,221	15,010,597	4,429,624
1990	65,559,187	28,815,650	36,743,537	45,796,700	31,445,600	14,351,100	19,762,487	14,638,613	5,123,874
1991	65,604,576	29,285,989	36,318,587	46,834,900	32,036,600	14,798,300	18,769,676	14,379,082	4,390,594
1992	68,556,330	30,400,953	38,155,377	47,491,489	32,029,400	15,462,089	21,064,841	15,892,444	5,172,397
1993	66,871,683	30,261,835	36,609,848	46,566,000	30,160,900	16,405,100	20,305,683	15,417,604	4,888,079
1994	68,485,265	30,810,468	37,674,797	47,842,373	31,147,921	16,694,452	20,642,892	15,931,569	4,711,323
1995	72,693,302	32,240,406	40,452,896	52,000,852	32,663,734	19,337,118	20,692,450	15,486,784	5,205,666
1996	68,523,616	29,387,127	39,136,489	49,551,012	31,380,213	18,170,799	18,972,604	14,676,617	4,295,987
1997	75,896,410	33,360,772	42,535,638	54,226,610	33,992,700	20,233,910	21,669,800	15,801,765	5,868,035
1998	74,671,801	31,698,781	42,973,020	52,732,954	34,170,744	18,562,210	21,938,847	16,411,582	5,527,265
1999	71,083,703	30,825,918	40,257,785	49,234,051	32,704,603	16,529,448	21,849,652	15,993,388	5,856,264
2000	66,636,782	29,556,605	37,080,177	44,377,350	29,406,351	14,970,999	22,259,432	16,191,336	6,068,096
2001	63,536,029	29,056,937	34,479,092	42,329,227	27,924,460	14,404,767	21,206,802	15,584,758	5,622,044
2002	63,810,921	28,814,604	34,996,317	42,090,354	28,436,938	13,653,416	21,720,567	15,634,848	6,085,719
2003	61,275,959	27,907,963	33,367,996	44,305,987	30,830,672	13,475,315	16,969,972	13,204,272	3,765,700
2004	63,813,020	28,883,098	34,929,922	46,972,355	32,305,334	14,667,021	16,840,665	13,352,498	3,488,167
2005	63,994,140	29,333,144	34,660,996	46,215,223	31,227,700	14,987,523	17,778,917	14,046,202	3,732,715
2006	64,685,448	29,824,319	34,861,129	46,338,727	31,730,076	14,608,651	18,346,721	14,293,473	4,053,248

Table A.1b—Pulpwood production in the South, by region and species group, 1953 to 2006

Year	Total southern production	Total Southeast	Total South Central	Roundwood			Residues		
				Total	Softwood	Hardwood	Total	Softwood	Hardwood
				green tons					
1953	43,926,056	23,932,181	19,993,875	43,740,719	38,198,461	5,542,258	185,337	65,871	119,466
1954	44,450,048	24,053,461	20,396,587	44,144,201	38,091,503	6,052,698	305,846	206,248	99,598
1955	49,798,922	27,828,553	21,970,369	48,892,225	41,816,863	7,075,362	906,697	622,830	283,867
1956	55,022,644	30,490,740	24,531,904	53,428,057	45,684,113	7,743,943	1,594,587	1,210,126	384,461
1957	53,353,570	29,652,230	23,701,340	50,451,591	42,426,774	8,024,817	2,901,979	2,545,387	356,592
1958	54,407,989	29,680,266	24,727,723	50,102,338	41,857,522	8,244,816	4,305,651	3,821,362	484,289
1959	61,092,835	34,005,360	27,087,475	55,154,844	44,591,774	10,563,070	5,937,991	5,258,316	679,674
1960	63,148,684	35,672,293	27,476,391	56,018,344	44,525,643	11,492,701	7,130,339	6,213,710	916,630
1961	64,914,589	36,522,945	28,391,644	56,921,143	44,606,449	12,314,694	7,993,446	6,811,528	1,181,918
1962	68,706,803	38,486,328	30,220,475	59,399,080	45,362,419	14,036,660	9,307,723	7,761,402	1,546,322
1963	71,339,843	39,909,331	31,430,512	61,031,540	46,303,966	14,727,574	10,308,303	8,517,596	1,790,707
1964	77,297,058	42,718,444	34,578,613	65,885,062	50,101,146	15,783,916	11,411,995	9,491,181	1,920,814
1965	82,544,786	45,303,167	37,241,619	70,016,197	52,711,139	17,305,058	12,528,589	10,288,412	2,240,177
1966	88,706,164	46,921,127	41,785,037	74,714,095	56,210,390	18,503,705	13,992,069	11,132,317	2,859,752
1967	90,087,687	47,278,273	42,809,414	74,246,210	56,139,990	18,106,220	15,841,477	12,391,827	3,449,649
1968	99,134,334	49,535,075	49,599,259	80,599,265	60,341,225	20,258,039	18,535,069	14,778,725	3,756,344
1969	109,227,654	52,780,498	56,447,156	88,815,694	66,104,216	22,711,478	20,411,961	16,001,615	4,410,346
1970	112,794,212	54,729,040	58,065,172	91,670,482	69,788,331	21,882,151	21,123,730	15,811,206	5,312,524
1971	111,870,273	52,560,393	59,309,880	87,054,122	65,084,872	21,969,251	24,816,150	19,670,507	5,145,643
1972	118,162,973	55,057,461	63,105,511	91,471,522	67,039,753	24,431,770	26,691,451	21,371,345	5,320,106
1973	125,699,129	58,006,240	67,692,889	94,352,937	68,292,318	26,060,619	31,346,192	24,733,766	6,612,427
1974	130,744,173	59,426,035	71,318,138	97,476,270	70,781,356	26,694,914	33,267,902	25,019,763	8,248,139
1975	112,203,786	51,485,897	60,717,889	82,024,366	61,456,574	20,567,792	30,179,420	23,972,908	6,206,513
1976	125,148,842	57,245,729	67,903,113	87,462,924	63,699,380	23,763,544	37,685,918	30,304,811	7,381,107
1977	128,672,858	61,923,292	66,749,566	87,541,092	63,895,927	23,645,166	41,131,766	33,691,696	7,440,070
1978	133,571,670	63,401,923	70,169,747	92,275,309	65,117,639	27,157,670	41,296,361	33,309,926	7,986,435
1979	143,308,981	64,888,078	78,420,903	97,812,448	70,598,004	27,214,443	45,496,533	35,157,882	10,338,651
1980	144,141,694	65,138,629	79,003,065	101,023,512	73,665,256	27,358,257	43,118,182	32,430,297	10,687,885
1981	143,489,684	66,031,172	77,458,512	100,051,856	72,759,500	27,292,356	43,437,828	31,751,721	11,686,107
1982	138,212,194	64,853,161	73,359,033	96,883,458	69,184,738	27,698,720	41,328,736	31,278,182	10,050,554
1983	150,064,418	69,948,646	80,115,772	103,502,523	69,605,387	33,897,136	46,561,895	35,654,753	10,907,142
1984	155,506,573	72,404,045	83,102,527	106,085,237	71,460,851	34,624,386	49,421,336	37,109,994	12,311,341
1985	150,734,167	71,117,711	79,616,456	102,045,310	68,172,030	33,873,280	48,688,857	37,079,412	11,609,445
1986	160,247,375	74,032,200	86,215,175	110,989,479	73,279,947	37,709,532	49,257,897	37,447,096	11,810,801
1987	165,347,743	77,168,529	88,179,214	113,144,650	75,645,090	37,499,560	52,203,093	38,945,714	13,257,379
1988	164,768,669	75,569,668	89,199,001	113,870,760	74,690,640	39,180,120	50,897,909	37,496,165	13,401,744
1989	162,053,889	73,371,332	88,682,557	115,034,380	74,268,900	40,765,480	47,019,509	36,100,486	10,919,023
1990	172,922,414	76,096,867	96,825,547	125,086,200	84,903,120	40,183,080	47,836,214	35,205,864	12,630,349
1991	173,338,566	77,511,388	95,827,178	127,934,060	86,498,820	41,435,240	45,404,506	34,581,692	10,822,814
1992	180,744,516	80,325,151	100,419,364	129,773,229	86,479,380	43,293,849	50,971,286	38,221,328	12,749,959
1993	176,497,162	80,267,821	96,229,341	127,368,710	81,434,430	45,934,280	49,128,452	37,079,338	12,049,115
1994	180,772,687	81,511,674	99,261,013	130,843,852	84,099,387	46,744,466	49,928,835	38,315,423	11,613,411
1995	192,413,694	85,447,564	106,966,131	142,336,012	88,192,082	54,143,930	50,077,682	37,245,716	12,831,967
1996	181,491,684	77,863,918	103,627,767	135,604,812	84,726,575	50,878,237	45,886,872	35,297,264	10,589,608
1997	200,903,189	88,247,100	112,656,089	148,435,238	91,780,290	56,654,948	52,467,951	38,003,245	14,464,706
1998	197,329,760	83,797,178	113,532,582	144,235,197	92,261,009	51,974,188	53,094,563	39,469,855	13,624,708
1999	187,484,671	81,386,908	106,097,763	134,584,883	88,302,428	46,282,454	52,899,789	38,464,098	14,435,691
2000	175,213,965	77,937,570	97,276,394	121,315,945	79,397,148	41,918,797	53,898,020	38,940,163	14,957,857
2001	167,069,071	76,360,087	90,708,985	115,729,390	75,396,042	40,333,348	51,339,681	37,481,343	13,858,338
2002	167,612,404	75,735,397	91,877,007	115,009,297	76,779,733	38,229,565	52,603,107	37,601,809	15,001,297
2003	162,012,421	73,997,938	88,014,483	120,973,696	83,242,814	37,730,882	41,038,725	31,756,274	9,282,451
2004	169,003,150	76,511,024	92,492,126	128,292,061	87,224,402	41,067,659	40,711,089	32,112,758	8,598,332
2005	169,262,113	77,388,176	91,873,937	126,279,854	84,314,790	41,965,064	42,982,258	33,781,116	9,201,142
2006	170,942,487	78,654,573	92,287,914	126,575,428	85,671,205	40,904,223	44,367,059	34,375,803	9,991,256

Table A.1c—Pulpwood production in the South, by region and species group, 1953 to 2006

Year	Total southern production	Total Southeast	Total South Central	Roundwood Total	Roundwood Softwood	Roundwood Hardwood	Residues Total	Residues Softwood	Residues Hardwood
				thousand cubic feet					
1953	1,202,258	645,020	557,238	1,197,202	1,045,741	151,461	5,056	1,802	3,254
1954	1,215,587	647,169	568,418	1,207,238	1,041,920	165,319	8,349	5,639	2,710
1955	1,360,501	748,220	612,281	1,335,780	1,142,316	193,463	24,722	17,014	7,708
1956	1,511,946	828,346	683,600	1,467,838	1,256,537	211,301	44,108	33,521	10,587
1957	1,487,813	818,827	668,987	1,407,474	1,182,583	224,890	80,340	70,431	9,909
1958	1,493,688	796,781	696,907	1,375,070	1,151,691	223,379	118,618	105,398	13,220
1959	1,666,219	895,432	770,787	1,501,878	1,215,589	286,288	164,341	145,925	18,417
1960	1,720,870	939,551	781,319	1,524,159	1,212,931	311,228	196,712	172,073	24,639
1961	1,764,120	955,681	808,439	1,542,847	1,206,758	336,090	221,273	189,138	32,135
1962	1,866,971	1,007,326	859,645	1,609,468	1,226,178	383,290	257,503	215,592	41,911
1963	1,955,037	1,043,798	911,239	1,666,996	1,262,544	404,452	288,041	239,073	48,968
1964	2,139,667	1,116,720	1,022,948	1,816,825	1,382,377	434,448	322,842	270,326	52,517
1965	2,285,765	1,184,835	1,100,930	1,931,372	1,451,828	479,544	354,393	293,277	61,116
1966	2,466,753	1,230,721	1,236,032	2,068,064	1,555,158	512,905	398,689	319,862	78,827
1967	2,511,953	1,244,494	1,267,459	2,059,867	1,558,991	500,876	452,086	356,828	95,258
1968	2,825,964	1,357,480	1,468,484	2,295,805	1,733,738	562,067	530,159	425,773	104,386
1969	3,094,119	1,423,327	1,670,792	2,509,214	1,892,072	617,142	584,905	462,028	122,877
1970	3,241,377	1,521,933	1,719,444	2,635,001	2,027,286	607,714	606,376	458,085	148,291
1971	3,223,254	1,466,523	1,756,731	2,510,513	1,894,584	615,928	712,742	569,324	143,418
1972	3,379,416	1,545,038	1,834,378	2,610,563	1,927,988	682,575	768,853	620,418	148,435
1973	3,595,817	1,627,589	1,968,228	2,691,568	1,963,218	728,350	904,249	719,046	185,203
1974	3,732,990	1,681,973	2,051,017	2,772,209	2,025,012	747,198	960,781	730,500	230,281
1975	3,194,488	1,457,117	1,737,371	2,322,942	1,748,771	574,171	871,546	697,046	174,500
1976	3,612,408	1,671,635	1,940,773	2,527,035	1,857,143	669,892	1,085,372	878,480	206,892
1977	3,703,883	1,805,570	1,898,313	2,520,544	1,857,189	663,356	1,183,338	973,584	209,754
1978	3,857,614	1,861,770	1,995,844	2,663,877	1,898,335	765,542	1,193,737	968,234	225,503
1979	4,143,048	1,912,287	2,230,761	2,830,692	2,054,129	776,563	1,312,356	1,020,355	292,001
1980	4,221,066	1,978,900	2,242,166	2,969,849	2,191,795	778,054	1,251,217	949,260	301,957
1981	4,213,934	2,016,655	2,197,279	2,952,537	2,176,746	775,791	1,261,397	930,624	330,773
1982	4,044,830	1,971,362	2,073,468	2,833,493	2,054,615	778,878	1,211,337	927,407	283,931
1983	4,387,672	2,126,403	2,261,268	3,021,232	2,074,261	946,971	1,366,440	1,058,374	308,066
1984	4,525,651	2,188,912	2,336,739	3,079,168	2,109,921	969,247	1,446,483	1,099,201	347,282
1985	4,359,947	2,127,174	2,232,773	2,935,171	1,990,998	944,173	1,424,776	1,097,423	327,353
1986	4,623,622	2,205,423	2,418,199	3,192,857	2,137,825	1,055,031	1,430,765	1,099,158	331,607
1987	4,751,124	2,297,253	2,453,871	3,246,853	2,212,900	1,033,953	1,504,271	1,134,412	369,859
1988	4,697,672	2,240,158	2,457,514	3,246,644	2,167,370	1,079,274	1,451,028	1,079,404	371,625
1989	4,583,614	2,142,000	2,441,614	3,253,723	2,132,491	1,121,232	1,329,892	1,026,360	303,532
1990	4,868,078	2,212,786	2,655,292	3,524,798	2,413,255	1,111,543	1,343,280	993,641	349,639
1991	4,881,725	2,264,784	2,616,941	3,610,285	2,472,069	1,138,216	1,271,440	971,978	299,462
1992	5,016,921	2,279,681	2,737,240	3,595,929	2,410,691	1,185,238	1,420,992	1,070,119	350,873
1993	4,886,277	2,263,929	2,622,348	3,521,511	2,265,563	1,255,948	1,364,766	1,033,200	331,565
1994	5,006,426	2,303,363	2,703,063	3,619,197	2,339,699	1,279,497	1,387,230	1,067,793	319,437
1995	5,266,555	2,360,268	2,906,287	3,881,747	2,404,076	1,477,671	1,384,808	1,031,982	352,826
1996	4,965,290	2,150,303	2,814,987	3,698,312	2,311,338	1,386,974	1,266,978	976,720	290,258
1997	5,501,157	2,427,030	3,074,127	4,065,082	2,521,006	1,544,075	1,436,076	1,040,833	395,243
1998	5,401,995	2,304,896	3,097,099	3,948,388	2,531,743	1,416,645	1,453,607	1,080,502	373,105
1999	5,111,548	2,225,635	2,885,913	3,664,013	2,406,096	1,257,917	1,447,535	1,053,746	393,789
2000	4,776,327	2,133,845	2,642,482	3,302,442	2,164,445	1,137,997	1,473,886	1,066,124	407,761
2001	4,551,387	2,086,046	2,465,341	3,149,114	2,051,847	1,097,267	1,402,273	1,024,398	377,875
2002	4,567,675	2,065,693	2,501,982	3,135,195	2,094,343	1,040,853	1,432,479	1,024,851	407,628
2003	4,408,250	2,010,176	2,398,074	3,288,690	2,263,389	1,025,300	1,119,560	865,974	253,586
2004	4,593,696	2,076,584	2,517,112	3,484,498	2,371,108	1,113,390	1,109,197	874,522	234,676
2005	4,602,280	2,109,811	2,492,470	3,426,929	2,290,665	1,136,263	1,175,352	924,296	251,055
2006	4,646,102	2,144,119	2,501,983	3,435,270	2,328,046	1,107,225	1,210,831	938,587	272,245

Table A.2a—Trends in pulpwood production in the Southeast, by species group, 1953 to 2006

Year	Total production	Roundwood			Residues		
		Total	Softwood	Hardwood	Total	Softwood	Hardwood
				standard cords			
1953	8,837,840	8,796,465	7,990,143	806,322	41,375	14,939	26,436
1954	8,884,130	8,815,768	7,964,138	851,630	68,362	46,468	21,894
1955	10,291,065	10,081,686	9,075,912	1,005,774	209,379	144,931	64,448
1956	11,272,250	11,079,034	9,983,131	1,095,903	193,216	141,994	51,222
1957	10,983,756	10,557,147	9,366,714	1,190,433	426,609	378,355	48,254
1958	11,021,489	10,289,057	8,944,966	1,344,091	732,432	667,371	65,061
1959	12,656,064	11,521,664	9,904,963	1,616,701	1,134,400	1,018,316	116,084
1960	13,303,645	11,839,007	10,108,934	1,730,073	1,464,638	1,272,768	191,870
1961	13,630,816	11,971,636	10,034,432	1,937,204	1,659,180	1,401,190	257,990
1962	14,380,875	12,436,692	10,333,845	2,102,847	1,944,183	1,590,609	353,574
1963	14,924,469	12,784,157	10,575,290	2,208,867	2,140,312	1,744,147	396,165
1964	15,972,302	13,683,593	11,254,138	2,429,455	2,288,709	1,864,501	424,208
1965	16,942,123	14,479,753	11,925,587	2,554,166	2,462,370	1,955,411	506,959
1966	17,560,369	14,850,509	12,161,353	2,689,156	2,709,860	2,066,123	643,737
1967	17,715,229	14,730,738	11,919,223	2,811,515	2,984,491	2,210,695	773,796
1968	18,588,225	15,189,437	12,130,735	3,058,702	3,398,788	2,671,464	727,324
1969	19,788,684	16,294,109	12,928,321	3,365,788	3,494,575	2,738,376	756,199
1970	20,517,428	16,954,807	13,645,713	3,309,094	3,562,621	2,695,148	867,473
1971	19,793,773	15,522,916	12,307,802	3,215,114	4,270,857	3,344,235	926,622
1972	20,745,072	16,153,507	12,715,847	3,437,660	4,591,565	3,649,686	941,879
1973	21,893,028	16,700,808	13,075,735	3,625,073	5,192,220	4,121,193	1,071,027
1974	22,485,394	16,660,553	13,194,914	3,465,639	5,824,841	4,370,926	1,453,915
1975	19,514,653	14,227,010	11,326,165	2,900,845	5,287,643	4,185,905	1,101,738
1976	21,778,823	15,088,246	11,689,609	3,398,637	6,690,577	5,411,188	1,279,389
1977	23,631,324	15,750,867	12,116,144	3,634,723	7,880,457	6,547,468	1,332,989
1978	24,154,458	16,357,490	12,396,945	3,960,545	7,796,968	6,314,680	1,482,288
1979	24,780,111	16,350,543	12,802,149	3,548,394	8,429,568	6,535,211	1,894,357
1980	24,805,820	16,974,948	13,256,469	3,718,479	7,830,872	6,144,625	1,686,247
1981	25,090,332	17,539,172	13,349,813	4,189,359	7,551,160	5,952,294	1,598,866
1982	24,615,865	17,441,023	13,221,500	4,219,523	7,174,842	5,758,976	1,415,866
1983	26,617,509	18,119,841	13,358,770	4,761,071	8,497,668	6,629,721	1,867,947
1984	27,569,807	18,649,946	13,796,512	4,853,434	8,919,861	7,060,160	1,859,701
1985	27,096,107	18,164,324	13,262,535	4,901,789	8,931,783	7,216,461	1,715,322
1986	28,132,108	19,467,269	14,064,687	5,402,582	8,664,839	7,141,875	1,522,964
1987	29,359,580	20,184,929	14,997,696	5,187,233	9,174,651	7,750,293	1,424,358
1988	28,698,590	20,017,398	14,476,953	5,540,445	8,681,192	7,174,828	1,506,364
1989	27,854,623	19,513,681	14,197,593	5,316,088	8,340,942	6,793,953	1,546,989
1990	28,815,650	20,886,164	15,408,652	5,477,512	7,929,486	6,495,172	1,434,314
1991	29,285,989	21,727,351	16,016,967	5,710,384	7,558,638	5,925,676	1,632,962
1992	30,400,953	22,120,164	16,255,570	5,864,594	8,280,789	6,631,594	1,649,195
1993	30,261,835	22,701,844	15,648,951	7,052,893	7,559,991	6,130,414	1,429,577
1994	30,810,468	22,540,109	15,828,406	6,711,703	8,270,359	6,737,093	1,533,266
1995	32,240,406	23,896,419	16,434,674	7,461,745	8,343,987	6,447,831	1,896,156
1996	29,387,127	21,858,287	15,335,299	6,522,988	7,528,840	6,072,445	1,456,395
1997	33,360,772	23,994,268	16,376,017	7,618,251	9,366,504	6,461,354	2,905,150
1998	31,698,781	22,747,118	15,728,985	7,018,133	8,951,663	6,461,718	2,489,945
1999	30,825,918	21,824,214	15,337,804	6,486,410	9,001,704	6,271,853	2,729,851
2000	29,556,605	20,655,155	14,627,475	6,027,680	8,901,450	6,269,841	2,631,609
2001	29,056,937	19,410,281	13,644,185	5,766,096	9,646,656	6,721,480	2,925,176
2002	28,814,604	19,407,349	14,101,668	5,305,681	9,407,255	6,398,284	3,008,971
2003	27,907,963	21,193,156	15,748,761	5,444,395	6,714,807	5,333,697	1,381,110
2004	28,883,098	21,637,873	16,021,189	5,616,684	7,245,225	5,539,682	1,705,543
2005	29,333,144	20,881,325	15,197,492	5,683,833	8,451,819	6,558,646	1,893,173
2006	29,824,319	21,166,236	15,596,432	5,569,804	8,658,083	6,556,989	2,101,094

Table A.2b—Trends in pulpwood production in the Southeast, by species group, 1953 to 2006

Year	Total production	Roundwood Total	Roundwood Softwood	Roundwood Hardwood	Residues Total	Residues Softwood	Residues Hardwood
				green tons			
1953	23,932,181	23,831,088	21,573,386	2,257,702	101,093	35,928	65,165
1954	24,053,461	23,887,737	21,503,173	2,384,564	165,724	111,756	53,969
1955	27,828,553	27,321,130	24,504,962	2,816,167	507,423	348,559	158,864
1956	30,490,740	30,022,982	26,954,454	3,068,528	467,758	341,496	126,262
1957	29,652,230	28,623,340	25,290,128	3,333,212	1,028,890	909,944	118,946
1958	29,680,266	27,914,863	24,151,408	3,763,455	1,765,403	1,605,027	160,375
1959	34,005,360	31,270,163	26,743,400	4,526,763	2,735,197	2,449,050	286,147
1960	35,672,293	32,138,326	27,294,122	4,844,204	3,533,967	3,061,007	472,960
1961	36,522,945	32,517,138	27,092,966	5,424,171	4,005,807	3,369,862	635,945
1962	38,486,328	33,789,353	27,901,382	5,887,972	4,696,975	3,825,415	871,560
1963	39,909,331	34,738,111	28,553,283	6,184,828	5,171,220	4,194,674	976,547
1964	42,718,444	37,188,647	30,386,173	6,802,474	5,529,798	4,484,125	1,045,673
1965	45,303,167	39,350,750	32,199,085	7,151,665	5,952,417	4,702,763	1,249,654
1966	46,921,127	40,365,290	32,835,653	7,529,637	6,555,838	4,969,026	1,586,812
1967	47,278,273	40,054,144	32,181,902	7,872,242	7,224,129	5,316,721	1,907,407
1968	49,535,075	41,317,350	32,752,985	8,564,366	8,217,725	6,424,871	1,792,854
1969	52,780,498	44,330,673	34,906,467	9,424,206	8,449,825	6,585,794	1,864,031
1970	54,729,040	46,108,888	36,843,425	9,265,463	8,620,152	6,481,831	2,138,321
1971	52,560,393	42,233,385	33,231,065	9,002,319	10,327,008	8,042,885	2,284,123
1972	55,057,461	43,958,235	34,332,787	9,625,448	11,099,227	8,777,495	2,321,732
1973	58,006,240	45,454,689	35,304,485	10,150,204	12,551,551	9,911,469	2,640,082
1974	59,426,035	45,330,057	35,626,268	9,703,789	14,095,978	10,512,077	3,583,900
1975	51,485,897	38,703,012	30,580,646	8,122,366	12,782,886	10,067,102	2,715,784
1976	57,245,729	41,078,128	31,561,944	9,516,184	16,167,601	13,013,907	3,153,694
1977	61,923,292	42,890,813	32,713,589	10,177,224	19,032,478	15,746,661	3,285,818
1978	63,401,923	44,561,278	33,471,752	11,089,526	18,840,645	15,186,805	3,653,840
1979	64,888,078	44,501,306	34,565,802	9,935,503	20,386,772	15,717,182	4,669,590
1980	65,138,629	46,204,208	35,792,466	10,411,741	18,934,422	14,777,823	4,156,599
1981	66,031,172	47,774,700	36,044,495	11,730,205	18,256,472	14,315,267	3,941,205
1982	64,853,161	47,512,714	35,698,050	11,814,664	17,340,447	13,850,337	3,490,110
1983	69,948,646	49,399,678	36,068,679	13,330,999	20,548,968	15,944,479	4,604,489
1984	72,404,045	50,840,198	37,250,582	13,589,615	21,563,848	16,979,685	4,584,163
1985	71,117,711	49,533,854	35,808,845	13,725,009	21,583,857	17,355,589	4,228,269
1986	74,032,200	53,101,885	37,974,655	15,127,230	20,930,316	17,176,209	3,754,106
1987	77,168,529	55,018,032	40,493,779	14,524,252	22,150,497	18,639,455	3,511,042
1988	75,569,668	54,601,019	39,087,773	15,513,246	20,968,649	17,255,461	3,713,187
1989	73,371,332	53,218,548	38,333,501	14,885,046	20,152,785	16,339,457	3,813,328
1990	76,096,867	56,940,394	41,603,360	15,337,034	19,156,473	15,620,889	3,535,584
1991	77,511,388	59,234,886	43,245,811	15,989,075	18,276,502	14,251,251	4,025,251
1992	80,325,151	60,310,902	43,890,039	16,420,863	20,014,249	15,948,984	4,065,266
1993	80,267,821	62,000,268	42,252,168	19,748,100	18,267,553	14,743,646	3,523,907
1994	81,511,674	61,529,465	42,736,696	18,792,768	19,982,209	16,202,709	3,779,501
1995	85,447,564	65,266,506	44,373,620	20,892,886	20,181,058	15,507,034	4,674,025
1996	77,863,918	59,669,674	41,405,307	18,264,366	18,194,244	14,604,230	3,590,014
1997	88,247,100	65,546,349	44,215,246	21,331,103	22,700,751	15,539,556	7,161,195
1998	83,797,178	62,119,032	42,468,260	19,650,772	21,678,146	15,540,432	6,137,714
1999	81,386,908	59,574,019	41,412,071	18,161,948	21,812,889	15,083,806	6,729,083
2000	77,937,570	56,371,687	39,494,183	16,877,504	21,565,884	15,078,968	6,486,916
2001	76,360,087	52,984,368	36,839,300	16,145,069	23,375,718	16,165,159	7,210,559
2002	75,735,397	52,930,410	38,074,504	14,855,907	22,804,987	15,387,873	7,417,114
2003	73,997,938	57,765,961	42,521,655	15,244,306	16,231,977	12,827,541	3,404,436
2004	76,511,024	58,983,926	43,257,210	15,726,715	17,527,099	13,322,935	4,204,163
2005	77,388,176	56,947,961	41,033,228	15,914,732	20,440,215	15,773,544	4,666,671
2006	78,654,573	57,705,818	42,110,366	15,595,451	20,948,755	15,769,559	5,179,197

9

Table A.2c—Trends in pulpwood production in the Southeast, by species group, 1953 to 2006

Year	Total production	Roundwood Total	Roundwood Softwood	Roundwood Hardwood	Residues Total	Residues Softwood	Residues Hardwood
		thousand cubic feet					
1953	645,020	642,300	582,139	60,161	2,720	968	1,752
1954	647,169	642,716	579,358	63,358	4,452	3,005	1,447
1955	748,220	734,603	659,485	75,118	13,617	9,367	4,250
1956	828,346	815,627	734,163	81,464	12,719	9,305	3,414
1957	818,827	790,934	698,017	92,917	27,892	24,675	3,217
1958	796,781	749,298	651,700	97,598	47,483	43,332	4,151
1959	895,432	822,634	705,727	116,907	72,798	65,369	7,429
1960	939,551	845,687	720,780	124,907	93,864	81,601	12,263
1961	955,681	848,498	705,885	142,613	107,182	90,278	16,904
1962	1,007,326	881,671	727,043	154,628	125,654	102,538	23,116
1963	1,043,798	905,426	743,025	162,401	138,372	112,512	25,859
1964	1,116,720	968,858	790,987	177,870	147,862	120,355	27,507
1965	1,184,835	1,026,054	836,551	189,504	158,781	125,974	32,808
1966	1,230,721	1,053,304	853,960	199,345	177,417	134,979	42,439
1967	1,244,494	1,048,744	840,278	208,466	195,749	144,594	51,155
1968	1,357,480	1,134,071	906,119	227,952	223,409	175,169	48,240
1969	1,423,327	1,193,665	956,169	237,496	229,662	179,578	50,084
1970	1,521,933	1,286,183	1,038,963	247,221	235,749	178,218	57,531
1971	1,466,523	1,184,411	938,996	245,414	282,112	220,522	61,590
1972	1,545,038	1,232,511	969,721	262,791	312,527	249,361	63,166
1973	1,627,589	1,273,830	996,807	277,023	353,758	281,639	72,120
1974	1,681,973	1,274,490	1,008,021	266,469	407,483	307,836	99,647
1975	1,457,117	1,087,032	864,032	223,000	370,085	294,529	75,556
1976	1,671,635	1,203,304	935,343	267,961	468,331	381,140	87,191
1977	1,805,570	1,252,411	968,854	283,557	553,159	461,029	92,130
1978	1,861,770	1,309,420	996,931	312,490	552,349	449,709	102,640
1979	1,912,287	1,316,290	1,027,121	289,169	595,997	464,789	131,207
1980	1,978,900	1,417,624	1,116,570	301,054	561,276	443,648	117,628
1981	2,016,655	1,474,041	1,136,075	337,965	542,614	430,254	112,360
1982	1,971,362	1,444,618	1,107,524	337,094	526,744	427,416	99,328
1983	2,126,403	1,502,870	1,127,792	375,078	623,534	493,145	130,389
1984	2,188,912	1,535,513	1,148,914	386,599	653,399	523,368	130,030
1985	2,127,174	1,473,963	1,090,742	383,221	653,211	533,396	119,815
1986	2,205,423	1,575,476	1,149,362	426,114	629,947	524,155	105,792
1987	2,297,253	1,637,003	1,236,311	400,692	660,251	561,526	98,725
1988	2,240,158	1,615,255	1,186,079	429,175	624,903	520,525	104,378
1989	2,142,000	1,553,963	1,143,063	410,900	588,037	480,859	107,178
1990	2,212,786	1,658,649	1,228,748	429,901	554,137	455,532	98,605
1991	2,264,784	1,737,811	1,295,955	441,856	526,973	415,058	111,915
1992	2,279,681	1,705,939	1,255,098	450,841	573,742	461,437	112,305
1993	2,263,929	1,744,588	1,204,094	540,495	519,341	422,330	97,010
1994	2,303,363	1,735,943	1,219,678	516,265	567,420	463,494	103,926
1995	2,360,268	1,791,030	1,222,614	568,416	569,238	440,265	128,973
1996	2,150,303	1,637,688	1,141,780	495,908	512,615	413,906	98,709
1997	2,427,030	1,801,078	1,223,405	577,673	625,952	430,604	195,348
1998	2,304,896	1,706,360	1,173,998	532,363	598,536	430,151	168,384
1999	2,225,635	1,625,534	1,135,143	490,391	600,101	417,460	182,641
2000	2,133,845	1,540,296	1,082,631	457,665	593,549	416,806	176,744
2001	2,086,046	1,444,881	1,006,271	438,609	641,165	444,560	196,605
2002	2,065,693	1,443,560	1,039,906	403,654	622,133	421,185	200,948
2003	2,010,176	1,566,630	1,154,293	412,337	443,546	350,879	92,667
2004	2,076,584	1,598,788	1,174,235	424,552	477,797	363,505	114,292
2005	2,109,811	1,547,428	1,118,809	428,619	562,382	434,892	127,490
2006	2,144,119	1,568,708	1,148,688	420,021	575,411	434,229	141,182

Table A.3a—Trends in pulpwood production in the South Central, by species group, 1953 to 2006

Year	Total production	Roundwood Total	Softwood	Hardwood	Residues Total	Softwood	Hardwood
				standard cords			
1953	7,364,970	7,330,491	6,157,435	1,173,056	34,479	12,450	22,029
1954	7,511,675	7,453,874	6,143,826	1,310,048	57,801	39,290	18,511
1955	8,097,709	7,932,956	6,411,815	1,521,141	164,753	114,042	50,711
1956	9,072,625	8,606,702	6,936,911	1,669,791	465,923	361,177	104,746
1957	8,798,905	8,022,479	6,346,906	1,675,573	776,426	680,018	96,408
1958	9,211,264	8,158,306	6,557,820	1,600,486	1,052,958	921,553	131,405
1959	10,094,073	8,766,333	6,610,509	2,155,824	1,327,740	1,168,094	159,646
1960	10,247,391	8,756,508	6,382,045	2,374,463	1,490,883	1,310,895	179,988
1961	10,599,912	8,947,376	6,486,475	2,460,901	1,652,536	1,431,046	221,490
1962	11,287,619	9,377,297	6,467,051	2,910,246	1,910,322	1,636,585	273,737
1963	11,753,069	9,625,308	6,574,327	3,050,981	2,127,761	1,797,473	330,288
1964	12,946,463	10,509,500	7,301,842	3,207,658	2,436,963	2,081,936	355,027
1965	13,947,619	11,223,269	7,597,057	3,626,212	2,724,350	2,322,515	401,835
1966	15,655,725	12,576,620	8,657,310	3,919,310	3,079,105	2,562,699	516,406
1967	16,095,846	12,528,358	8,873,366	3,654,992	3,567,488	2,941,832	625,656
1968	18,664,263	14,394,179	10,217,867	4,176,312	4,270,084	3,473,536	796,548
1969	21,248,266	16,300,176	11,554,722	4,745,454	4,948,090	3,915,102	1,032,988
1970	21,874,644	16,707,777	12,201,817	4,505,960	5,166,867	3,879,158	1,287,709
1971	22,424,383	16,428,753	11,797,706	4,631,047	5,995,630	4,834,770	1,160,860
1972	23,854,570	17,401,663	12,113,691	5,287,972	6,452,907	5,236,528	1,216,379
1973	25,674,623	17,900,007	12,217,716	5,682,291	7,774,616	6,163,117	1,611,499
1974	27,013,150	19,088,662	13,020,403	6,068,259	7,924,488	6,032,302	1,892,186
1975	23,078,481	15,880,324	11,435,529	4,444,795	7,198,157	5,782,040	1,416,117
1976	25,895,637	16,991,097	11,902,754	5,088,343	8,904,540	7,189,565	1,714,975
1977	25,505,841	16,358,993	11,549,014	4,809,979	9,146,848	7,461,553	1,685,295
1978	26,752,568	17,459,322	11,720,699	5,738,623	9,293,246	7,535,601	1,757,645
1979	29,899,583	19,516,310	13,345,260	6,171,050	10,383,273	8,083,451	2,299,822
1980	30,068,801	20,079,286	14,026,959	6,052,327	9,989,515	7,339,906	2,649,609
1981	29,548,094	19,156,061	13,598,150	5,557,911	10,392,033	7,250,085	3,141,948
1982	27,983,297	18,075,354	12,402,477	5,672,877	9,907,943	7,246,505	2,661,438
1983	30,518,449	19,766,052	12,421,003	7,345,049	10,752,397	8,195,540	2,556,857
1984	31,687,837	20,182,888	12,670,470	7,512,418	11,504,949	8,370,191	3,134,758
1985	30,377,742	19,182,176	11,986,365	7,195,811	11,195,566	8,201,174	2,994,392
1986	32,838,221	21,141,142	13,076,034	8,065,108	11,697,079	8,428,643	3,268,436
1987	33,621,711	21,224,471	13,019,004	8,205,467	12,397,240	8,443,351	3,953,889
1988	33,985,244	21,638,702	13,186,247	8,452,455	12,346,542	8,416,093	3,930,449
1989	33,651,698	22,552,419	13,309,407	9,243,012	11,099,279	8,216,644	2,882,635
1990	36,743,537	24,910,536	16,036,948	8,873,588	11,833,001	8,143,441	3,689,560
1991	36,318,587	25,107,549	16,019,633	9,087,916	11,211,038	8,453,406	2,757,632
1992	38,155,377	25,371,325	15,773,830	9,597,495	12,784,052	9,260,850	3,523,202
1993	36,609,848	23,864,156	14,511,949	9,352,207	12,745,692	9,287,190	3,458,502
1994	37,674,797	25,302,264	15,319,515	9,982,749	12,372,533	9,194,476	3,178,057
1995	40,452,896	28,104,433	16,229,060	11,875,373	12,348,463	9,038,953	3,309,510
1996	39,136,489	27,692,725	16,044,914	11,647,811	11,443,764	8,604,172	2,839,592
1997	42,535,638	30,232,342	17,616,683	12,615,659	12,303,296	9,340,411	2,962,885
1998	42,973,020	29,985,836	18,441,759	11,544,077	12,987,184	9,949,864	3,037,320
1999	40,257,785	27,409,837	17,366,799	10,043,038	12,847,948	9,721,535	3,126,413
2000	37,080,177	23,722,195	14,778,876	8,943,319	13,357,982	9,921,495	3,436,487
2001	34,479,092	22,918,946	14,280,275	8,638,671	11,560,146	8,863,278	2,696,868
2002	34,996,317	22,683,005	14,335,270	8,347,735	12,313,312	9,236,564	3,076,748
2003	33,367,996	23,112,831	15,081,911	8,030,920	10,255,165	7,870,575	2,384,590
2004	34,929,922	25,334,482	16,284,145	9,050,337	9,595,440	7,812,816	1,782,624
2005	34,660,996	25,333,898	16,030,208	9,303,690	9,327,098	7,487,556	1,839,542
2006	34,861,129	25,172,491	16,133,644	9,038,847	9,688,638	7,736,484	1,952,154

Table A.3b—Trends in pulpwood production in the South Central, by species group, 1953 to 2006

Year	Total production	Roundwood Total	Softwood	Hardwood	Residues Total	Softwood	Hardwood
				green tons			
1953	19,993,875	19,909,631	16,625,075	3,284,557	84,244	29,942	54,301
1954	20,396,587	20,256,465	16,588,330	3,668,134	140,122	94,492	45,630
1955	21,970,369	21,571,095	17,311,901	4,259,195	399,274	274,271	125,003
1956	24,531,904	23,405,075	18,729,660	4,675,415	1,126,830	868,631	258,199
1957	23,701,340	21,828,251	17,136,646	4,691,604	1,873,089	1,635,443	237,646
1958	24,727,723	22,187,475	17,706,114	4,481,361	2,540,248	2,216,335	323,913
1959	27,087,475	23,884,682	17,848,374	6,036,307	3,202,793	2,809,266	393,527
1960	27,476,391	23,880,018	17,231,522	6,648,496	3,596,373	3,152,702	443,670
1961	28,391,644	24,404,005	17,513,483	6,890,523	3,987,638	3,441,666	545,973
1962	30,220,475	25,609,727	17,461,038	8,148,689	4,610,749	3,935,987	674,762
1963	31,430,512	26,293,430	17,750,683	8,542,747	5,137,082	4,322,923	814,160
1964	34,578,613	28,696,416	19,714,973	8,981,442	5,882,198	5,007,056	875,142
1965	37,241,619	30,665,448	20,512,054	10,153,394	6,576,172	5,585,649	990,523
1966	41,785,037	34,348,805	23,374,737	10,974,068	7,436,232	6,163,291	1,272,941
1967	42,809,414	34,192,066	23,958,088	10,233,978	8,617,348	7,075,106	1,542,242
1968	49,599,259	39,281,915	27,588,241	11,693,674	10,317,345	8,353,854	1,963,491
1969	56,447,156	44,485,021	31,197,749	13,287,271	11,962,136	9,415,820	2,546,315
1970	58,065,172	45,561,594	32,944,906	12,616,688	12,503,578	9,329,375	3,174,203
1971	59,309,880	44,820,738	31,853,806	12,966,932	14,489,142	11,627,622	2,861,520
1972	63,105,511	47,513,287	32,706,966	14,806,322	15,592,224	12,593,850	2,998,374
1973	67,692,889	48,898,248	32,987,833	15,910,415	18,794,641	14,822,296	3,972,345
1974	71,318,138	52,146,213	35,155,088	16,991,125	19,171,925	14,507,686	4,664,238
1975	60,717,889	43,321,354	30,875,928	12,445,426	17,396,535	13,905,806	3,490,728
1976	67,903,113	46,384,796	32,137,436	14,247,360	21,518,317	17,290,904	4,227,413
1977	66,749,566	44,650,279	31,182,338	13,467,941	22,099,287	17,945,035	4,154,252
1978	70,169,747	47,714,032	31,645,887	16,068,144	22,455,715	18,123,120	4,332,595
1979	78,420,903	53,311,142	36,032,202	17,278,940	25,109,761	19,440,700	5,669,061
1980	79,003,065	54,819,305	37,872,789	16,946,516	24,183,760	17,652,474	6,531,286
1981	77,458,512	52,277,156	36,715,005	15,562,151	25,181,356	17,436,454	7,744,902
1982	73,359,033	49,370,744	33,486,688	15,884,056	23,988,289	17,427,845	6,560,445
1983	80,115,772	54,102,845	33,536,708	20,566,137	26,012,926	19,710,274	6,302,653
1984	83,102,527	55,245,039	34,210,269	21,034,770	27,857,488	20,130,309	7,727,178
1985	79,616,456	52,511,456	32,363,186	20,148,271	27,105,000	19,723,823	7,381,176
1986	86,215,175	57,887,594	35,305,292	22,582,302	28,327,581	20,270,886	8,056,695
1987	88,179,214	58,126,618	35,151,311	22,975,308	30,052,596	20,306,259	9,746,336
1988	89,199,001	59,269,741	35,602,867	23,666,874	29,929,260	20,240,704	9,688,557
1989	88,682,557	61,815,833	35,935,399	25,880,434	26,866,724	19,761,029	7,105,695
1990	96,825,547	68,145,806	43,299,760	24,846,046	28,679,741	19,584,976	9,094,765
1991	95,827,178	68,699,174	43,253,009	25,446,165	27,128,004	20,330,441	6,797,563
1992	100,419,364	69,462,327	42,589,341	26,872,986	30,957,037	22,272,344	8,684,693
1993	96,229,341	65,368,442	39,182,262	26,186,180	30,860,899	22,335,692	8,525,207
1994	99,261,013	69,314,388	41,362,691	27,951,697	29,946,625	22,112,715	7,833,911
1995	106,966,131	77,069,506	43,818,462	33,251,044	29,896,624	21,738,682	8,157,942
1996	103,627,767	75,935,139	43,321,268	32,613,871	27,692,628	20,693,034	6,999,594
1997	112,656,089	82,888,889	47,565,044	35,323,845	29,767,200	22,463,688	7,303,512
1998	113,532,582	82,116,165	49,792,749	32,323,416	31,416,417	23,929,423	7,486,994
1999	106,097,763	75,010,864	46,890,357	28,120,506	31,086,900	23,380,292	7,706,608
2000	97,276,394	64,944,258	39,902,965	25,041,293	32,332,136	23,861,195	8,470,940
2001	90,708,985	62,745,021	38,556,743	24,188,279	27,963,963	21,316,184	6,647,780
2002	91,877,007	62,078,887	38,705,229	23,373,658	29,798,120	22,213,936	7,584,184
2003	88,014,483	63,207,736	40,721,160	22,486,576	24,806,747	18,928,733	5,878,014
2004	92,492,126	69,308,135	43,967,192	25,340,944	23,183,991	18,789,822	4,394,168
2005	91,873,937	69,331,894	43,281,562	26,050,332	22,542,043	18,007,572	4,534,471
2006	92,287,914	68,869,610	43,560,839	25,308,772	23,418,304	18,606,244	4,812,060

Table A.3c—Trends in pulpwood production in the South Central, by species group, 1953 to 2006

Year	Total production	Roundwood			Residues		
		Total	Softwood	Hardwood	Total	Softwood	Hardwood
				thousand cubic feet			
1953	557,238	554,902	463,602	91,300	2,336	835	1,502
1954	568,418	564,522	462,561	101,961	3,896	2,634	1,262
1955	612,281	601,177	482,832	118,345	11,104	7,647	3,457
1956	683,600	652,211	522,374	129,837	31,389	24,216	7,173
1957	668,987	616,539	484,566	131,973	52,447	45,756	6,691
1958	696,907	625,772	499,991	125,781	71,135	62,066	9,068
1959	770,787	679,243	509,862	169,381	91,543	80,556	10,987
1960	781,319	678,472	492,151	186,320	102,847	90,471	12,376
1961	808,439	694,349	500,872	193,476	114,091	98,859	15,232
1962	859,645	727,797	499,135	228,661	131,849	113,054	18,794
1963	911,239	761,570	519,519	242,051	149,669	126,561	23,109
1964	1,022,948	847,968	591,389	256,578	174,980	149,970	25,010
1965	1,100,930	905,318	615,278	290,040	195,612	167,303	28,308
1966	1,236,032	1,014,759	701,199	313,561	221,272	184,884	36,389
1967	1,267,459	1,011,123	718,713	292,410	256,336	212,234	44,103
1968	1,468,484	1,161,734	827,619	334,115	306,750	250,604	56,145
1969	1,670,792	1,315,549	935,903	379,646	355,242	282,450	72,793
1970	1,719,444	1,348,818	988,324	360,494	370,626	279,867	90,760
1971	1,756,731	1,326,102	955,588	370,514	430,629	348,802	81,828
1972	1,834,378	1,378,052	958,267	419,784	456,326	371,057	85,269
1973	1,968,228	1,417,737	966,411	451,326	550,490	437,407	113,083
1974	2,051,017	1,497,719	1,016,991	480,728	553,297	422,663	130,634
1975	1,737,371	1,235,910	884,740	351,170	501,461	402,517	98,944
1976	1,940,773	1,323,732	921,801	401,931	617,041	497,340	119,701
1977	1,898,313	1,268,134	888,335	379,799	630,179	512,555	117,624
1978	1,995,844	1,354,457	901,405	453,052	641,388	518,525	122,863
1979	2,230,761	1,514,402	1,027,008	487,393	716,359	555,566	160,793
1980	2,242,166	1,552,225	1,075,226	477,000	689,941	505,612	184,329
1981	2,197,279	1,478,496	1,040,671	437,825	718,783	500,370	218,413
1982	2,073,468	1,388,875	947,091	441,784	684,594	499,991	184,603
1983	2,261,268	1,518,362	946,469	571,893	742,906	565,229	177,677
1984	2,336,739	1,543,655	961,007	582,648	793,085	575,833	217,251
1985	2,232,773	1,461,208	900,256	560,952	771,565	564,026	207,538
1986	2,418,199	1,617,380	988,463	628,917	800,818	575,003	225,815
1987	2,453,871	1,609,851	976,589	633,262	844,020	572,886	271,134
1988	2,457,514	1,631,389	981,290	650,099	826,125	558,879	267,246
1989	2,441,614	1,699,759	989,428	710,332	741,855	545,500	196,354
1990	2,655,292	1,866,150	1,184,508	681,642	789,143	538,109	251,033
1991	2,616,941	1,872,474	1,176,114	696,359	744,467	556,920	187,547
1992	2,737,240	1,889,990	1,155,593	734,396	847,250	608,682	238,568
1993	2,622,348	1,776,923	1,061,469	715,453	845,425	610,870	234,555
1994	2,703,063	1,883,253	1,120,022	763,232	819,810	604,299	215,511
1995	2,906,287	2,090,717	1,181,462	909,255	815,570	591,716	223,854
1996	2,814,987	2,060,624	1,169,558	891,066	754,363	562,813	191,550
1997	3,074,127	2,264,004	1,297,602	966,402	810,124	610,229	199,894
1998	3,097,099	2,242,028	1,357,746	884,283	855,071	650,350	204,721
1999	2,885,913	2,038,479	1,270,953	767,526	847,434	636,286	211,148
2000	2,642,482	1,762,146	1,081,814	680,332	880,336	649,319	231,018
2001	2,465,341	1,704,233	1,045,576	658,658	761,108	579,838	181,270
2002	2,501,982	1,691,635	1,054,437	637,199	810,346	603,666	206,680
2003	2,398,074	1,722,060	1,109,097	612,964	676,014	515,095	160,919
2004	2,517,112	1,885,711	1,196,873	688,838	631,401	511,016	120,384
2005	2,492,470	1,879,500	1,171,856	707,644	612,969	489,404	123,565
2006	2,501,983	1,866,562	1,179,358	687,204	635,421	504,358	131,063

Table A.4—Southern pulpmills and capacity, 1953 to 2006

Year	Total mills	Southern mills	Mills outside South	Southern pulpwood capacity	Average pulping capacity southern mills
	- - - - - - - *number* - - - - - - -			- - - - - *tons per 24 hours* - - - -	
1953	65	61	4	28,670	470
1954	71	67	4	32,376	483
1955	73	69	4	34,087	494
1956	72	68	4	38,332	564
1957	76	72	4	40,997	569
1958	80	75	5	44,502	593
1959	81	76	5	46,112	607
1960	88	81	7	50,313	621
1961	89	81	8	51,156	632
1962	89	80	9	52,146	652
1963	90	81	9	54,222	669
1964	93	82	11	56,530	689
1965	91	82	9	59,230	722
1966	97	87	10	64,726	744
1967	100	92	8	70,527	767
1968	113	101	12	77,390	766
1969	121	107	14	81,430	761
1970	119	110	9	84,366	767
1971	123	112	11	88,546	791
1972	124	110	14	88,724	807
1973	126	113	13	93,105	824
1974	127	116	11	95,882	827
1975	125	115	10	97,455	847
1976	122	114	8	98,974	868
1977	124	115	9	101,794	885
1978	125	115	10	104,030	905
1979	129	117	12	110,953	948
1980	127	116	11	112,827	973
1981	123	116	7	115,492	996
1982	115	112	3	117,933	1,053
1983	114	111	3	120,728	1,088
1984	113	110	3	121,408	1,104
1985	110	107	3	123,418	1,153
1986	110	107	3	121,535	1,136
1987	111	108	3	124,899	1,156
1988	110	108	2	127,977	1,185
1989	111	108	3	129,959	1,203
1990	108	105	3	131,000	1,248
1991	108	106	2	135,156	1,275
1992	107	105	2	135,275	1,288
1993	106	104	2	134,867	1,297
1994	109	104	5	139,880	1,345
1995	108	105	3	139,315	1,327
1996	108	105	3	137,160	1,306
1997	107	103	4	140,153	1,361
1998	107	103	4	140,610	1,365
1999	100	97	3	134,418	1,386
2000	101	98	3	130,337	1,330
2001	97	94	3	123,105	1,310
2002	95	92	3	127,110	1,382
2003	94	91	3	127,390	1,400
2004	92	89	3	125,182	1,407
2005	90	87	3	124,567	1,432
2006	90	87	3	125,093	1,438

Table A.5a—Trends in pulpwood production by species group, Alabama, 1953 to 2006

Year	Total production	Roundwood Total	Roundwood Softwood	Roundwood Hardwood	Residues Total	Residues Softwood	Residues Hardwood
				standard cords			
1953	1,773,520	1,765,140	1,726,196	38,944	8,380	3,026	5,354
1954	1,846,094	1,831,889	1,764,912	66,977	14,205	9,656	4,549
1955	1,968,886	1,928,828	1,860,115	68,713	40,058	27,728	12,330
1956	2,187,390	2,103,011	2,001,328	101,683	84,379	59,963	24,416
1957	2,294,189	2,134,367	1,997,190	137,177	159,822	136,438	23,384
1958	2,624,636	2,370,230	2,187,796	182,434	254,406	211,070	43,336
1959	2,930,962	2,582,142	2,150,704	431,438	348,820	294,456	54,364
1960	3,019,698	2,593,664	2,016,360	577,304	426,034	354,620	71,414
1961	3,300,392	2,805,599	2,168,848	636,751	494,793	395,959	98,834
1962	3,448,195	2,842,447	2,174,388	668,059	605,748	456,389	149,359
1963	3,649,835	3,014,130	2,325,130	689,000	635,705	477,403	158,302
1964	4,155,323	3,463,318	2,644,713	818,605	692,005	536,308	155,697
1965	4,862,808	4,068,619	3,032,994	1,035,625	794,189	600,873	193,316
1966	5,291,911	4,464,306	3,269,391	1,194,915	827,605	605,516	222,089
1967	5,633,972	4,781,346	3,625,974	1,155,372	852,626	654,583	198,043
1968	6,131,165	5,046,448	3,549,388	1,497,060	1,084,717	866,593	218,124
1969	6,378,707	5,135,721	3,556,619	1,579,102	1,242,986	964,678	278,308
1970	6,409,342	5,188,539	3,676,075	1,512,464	1,220,803	963,022	257,781
1971	6,283,546	4,858,671	3,429,940	1,428,731	1,424,875	1,157,292	267,583
1972	6,991,815	5,458,325	3,819,311	1,639,014	1,533,490	1,258,812	274,678
1973	7,172,192	5,511,158	3,864,629	1,646,529	1,661,034	1,352,217	308,817
1974	7,392,062	5,687,826	3,981,023	1,706,803	1,704,236	1,325,108	379,128
1975	6,334,964	4,668,167	3,402,583	1,265,584	1,666,797	1,377,919	288,878
1976	7,393,533	5,007,359	3,541,186	1,466,173	2,386,174	1,977,998	408,176
1977	7,072,084	4,793,643	3,392,969	1,400,674	2,278,441	1,916,217	362,224
1978	7,353,825	4,797,625	3,075,885	1,721,740	2,556,200	2,218,417	337,783
1979	8,220,872	5,606,161	3,782,223	1,823,938	2,614,711	2,145,114	469,597
1980	8,756,102	6,224,397	4,288,028	1,936,369	2,531,705	2,057,722	473,983
1981	8,644,319	6,400,013	4,515,913	1,884,100	2,244,306	1,727,984	516,322
1982	8,291,975	6,118,264	4,154,345	1,963,919	2,173,711	1,673,794	499,917
1983	8,988,715	6,693,499	4,153,089	2,540,410	2,295,216	1,867,109	428,107
1984	9,573,695	6,943,468	4,243,951	2,699,517	2,630,227	2,037,010	593,217
1985	9,056,671	6,759,733	4,046,897	2,712,836	2,296,938	1,811,421	485,517
1986	9,584,375	7,136,954	4,137,299	2,999,655	2,447,421	1,881,313	566,108
1987	9,322,004	7,061,404	3,972,432	3,088,972	2,260,600	1,661,508	599,092
1988	9,279,476	6,800,038	3,826,198	2,973,840	2,479,438	1,849,515	629,923
1989	8,441,986	6,555,890	3,412,998	3,142,892	1,886,096	1,550,387	335,709
1990	9,913,216	7,310,308	4,269,890	3,040,418	2,602,908	1,936,787	666,121
1991	9,919,358	7,646,280	4,326,880	3,319,400	2,273,078	1,992,382	280,696
1992	11,354,138	8,704,136	5,105,202	3,598,934	2,650,002	1,932,188	717,814
1993	10,328,443	8,002,132	4,699,962	3,302,170	2,326,311	1,839,198	487,113
1994	11,346,928	8,898,731	5,393,811	3,504,920	2,448,197	1,834,082	614,115
1995	11,712,350	9,415,097	5,723,612	3,691,485	2,297,253	1,726,142	571,111
1996	12,111,227	9,777,458	5,854,149	3,923,309	2,333,769	1,742,023	591,746
1997	13,054,905	10,155,271	6,209,332	3,945,939	2,899,634	2,125,588	774,046
1998	13,614,839	10,713,261	6,528,057	4,185,204	2,901,578	2,268,187	633,391
1999	11,650,922	8,662,811	5,709,427	2,953,384	2,988,111	2,269,816	718,295
2000	10,719,837	7,870,510	4,999,850	2,870,660	2,849,327	2,173,959	675,368
2001	10,163,644	7,527,211	5,014,584	2,512,627	2,636,433	1,914,571	721,862
2002	11,056,704	7,889,361	5,531,357	2,358,004	3,167,343	2,250,975	916,368
2003	9,389,605	7,031,710	4,665,659	2,366,051	2,357,895	1,749,324	608,571
2004	10,205,950	7,520,678	5,225,572	2,295,106	2,685,272	2,150,778	534,494
2005	10,212,005	7,652,384	5,134,274	2,518,110	2,559,621	1,999,299	560,322
2006	10,480,554	7,807,365	5,296,518	2,510,847	2,673,189	2,119,780	553,409

Table A.5b—Trends in pulpwood production by species group, Alabama, 1953 to 2006

Year	Total production	Roundwood Total	Softwood	Hardwood	Residues Total	Softwood	Hardwood
				green tons			
1953	4,790,248	4,769,772	4,660,729	109,043	20,475	7,278	13,198
1954	4,987,234	4,952,798	4,765,262	187,536	34,436	23,223	11,213
1955	5,311,786	5,214,707	5,022,311	192,396	97,079	66,686	30,393
1956	5,892,694	5,688,298	5,403,586	284,712	204,396	144,211	60,185
1957	6,162,284	5,776,509	5,392,413	384,096	385,775	328,133	57,642
1958	7,032,311	6,417,864	5,907,049	510,815	614,447	507,623	106,823
1959	7,857,101	7,014,927	5,806,901	1,208,026	842,174	708,167	134,007
1960	8,089,520	7,060,623	5,444,172	1,616,451	1,028,897	852,861	176,036
1961	8,834,700	7,638,792	5,855,890	1,782,903	1,195,907	952,281	243,626
1962	9,207,198	7,741,413	5,870,848	1,870,565	1,465,785	1,097,616	368,170
1963	9,745,420	8,207,051	6,277,851	1,929,200	1,538,369	1,148,154	390,214
1964	11,106,433	9,432,819	7,140,725	2,292,094	1,673,614	1,289,821	383,793
1965	13,010,457	11,088,834	8,189,084	2,899,750	1,921,624	1,445,100	476,524
1966	14,176,833	12,173,118	8,827,356	3,345,762	2,003,715	1,456,266	547,449
1967	15,087,620	13,025,171	9,790,130	3,235,042	2,062,448	1,574,272	488,176
1968	16,396,947	13,775,116	9,583,348	4,191,768	2,621,832	2,084,156	537,676
1969	17,030,437	14,024,357	9,602,871	4,421,486	3,006,080	2,320,051	686,029
1970	17,111,800	14,160,302	9,925,403	4,234,899	2,951,498	2,316,068	635,430
1971	16,704,164	13,261,285	9,260,838	4,000,447	3,442,879	2,783,287	659,592
1972	18,605,903	14,901,379	10,312,140	4,589,239	3,704,524	3,027,443	677,081
1973	19,058,095	15,044,780	10,434,498	4,610,281	4,013,316	3,252,082	761,234
1974	19,649,246	15,527,811	10,748,762	4,779,048	4,121,435	3,186,885	934,551
1975	16,756,589	12,730,609	9,186,974	3,543,635	4,025,979	3,313,895	712,084
1976	19,429,726	13,666,487	9,561,202	4,105,284	5,763,239	4,757,085	1,006,154
1977	18,584,288	13,082,904	9,161,016	3,921,887	5,501,384	4,608,502	892,882
1978	19,293,689	13,125,762	8,304,890	4,820,872	6,167,928	5,335,293	832,635
1979	21,635,584	15,319,029	10,212,002	5,107,026	6,316,556	5,158,999	1,157,557
1980	23,116,698	16,999,509	11,577,676	5,421,833	6,117,190	4,948,821	1,168,368
1981	22,896,980	17,468,445	12,192,965	5,275,480	5,428,535	4,155,802	1,272,734
1982	21,973,475	16,715,705	11,216,732	5,498,973	5,257,770	4,025,475	1,232,295
1983	23,872,169	18,326,488	11,213,340	7,113,148	5,545,681	4,490,397	1,055,284
1984	25,378,604	19,017,315	11,458,668	7,558,648	6,361,289	4,899,009	1,462,280
1985	24,075,830	18,522,563	10,926,622	7,595,941	5,553,267	4,356,468	1,196,799
1986	25,489,755	19,569,741	11,170,707	8,399,034	5,920,014	4,524,558	1,395,456
1987	24,847,377	19,374,688	10,725,566	8,649,122	5,472,689	3,995,927	1,476,762
1988	24,658,330	18,657,487	10,330,735	8,326,752	6,000,844	4,448,084	1,552,760
1989	22,571,396	18,015,192	9,215,095	8,800,098	4,556,203	3,728,681	827,523
1990	26,341,834	20,041,873	11,528,703	8,513,170	6,299,961	4,657,973	1,641,988
1991	26,460,490	20,976,896	11,682,576	9,294,320	5,483,594	4,791,679	691,916
1992	30,277,384	23,861,061	13,784,045	10,077,015	6,416,324	4,646,912	1,769,412
1993	27,559,978	21,935,973	12,689,897	9,246,076	5,624,005	4,423,271	1,200,734
1994	30,301,826	24,377,066	14,563,290	9,813,776	5,924,761	4,410,967	1,513,793
1995	31,349,071	25,789,910	15,453,752	10,336,158	5,559,160	4,151,372	1,407,789
1996	32,439,687	26,791,468	15,806,202	10,985,265	5,648,219	4,189,565	1,458,654
1997	34,833,888	27,813,826	16,765,196	11,048,629	7,020,063	5,112,039	1,908,023
1998	36,360,624	29,344,325	17,625,754	11,718,571	7,016,299	5,454,990	1,561,309
1999	30,914,433	23,684,928	15,415,453	8,269,475	7,229,505	5,458,907	1,770,597
2000	28,430,597	21,537,443	13,499,595	8,037,848	6,893,154	5,228,371	1,664,782
2001	26,958,665	20,574,732	13,539,377	7,035,356	6,383,933	4,604,543	1,779,390
2002	29,209,517	21,537,075	14,934,664	6,602,411	7,672,442	5,413,595	2,258,847
2003	24,929,474	19,222,222	12,597,279	6,624,943	5,707,252	4,207,124	1,500,128
2004	27,025,490	20,535,341	14,109,044	6,426,297	6,490,149	5,172,621	1,317,528
2005	27,102,756	20,913,248	13,862,540	7,050,708	6,189,508	4,808,314	1,381,194
2006	27,793,194	21,330,970	14,300,599	7,030,372	6,462,224	5,098,071	1,364,153

Table A.5c—Trends in pulpwood production by species group, Alabama, 1953 to 2006

Year	Total production	Roundwood			Residues		
		Total	Softwood	Hardwood	Total	Softwood	Hardwood
				thousand cubic feet			
1953	133,723	133,156	130,148	3,007	567	203	364
1954	139,197	138,239	133,067	5,172	958	648	309
1955	148,252	145,551	140,245	5,306	2,700	1,862	838
1956	164,431	158,744	150,892	7,852	5,687	4,027	1,660
1957	171,926	161,173	150,580	10,593	10,753	9,163	1,590
1958	196,160	179,039	164,951	14,088	17,121	14,175	2,946
1959	218,942	195,471	162,154	33,317	23,471	19,775	3,696
1960	225,277	196,607	152,025	44,581	28,671	23,816	4,855
1961	246,005	212,694	163,522	49,172	33,311	26,592	6,719
1962	256,334	215,530	163,940	51,590	40,804	30,650	10,154
1963	289,049	243,456	188,336	55,120	45,594	34,445	11,149
1964	329,370	279,710	214,222	65,488	49,660	38,695	10,966
1965	385,490	328,523	245,673	82,850	56,968	43,353	13,615
1966	419,743	360,414	264,821	95,593	59,329	43,688	15,641
1967	447,310	386,134	293,704	92,430	61,176	47,228	13,948
1968	485,152	407,265	287,500	119,765	77,887	62,525	15,362
1969	503,617	414,414	288,086	126,328	89,202	69,602	19,601
1970	506,396	418,759	297,762	120,997	87,637	69,482	18,155
1971	494,470	392,126	277,825	114,301	102,344	83,499	18,845
1972	517,249	414,291	286,448	127,843	102,957	84,096	18,862
1973	529,818	418,276	289,847	128,429	111,541	90,336	21,206
1974	546,266	431,707	298,577	133,131	114,559	88,525	26,034
1975	465,799	353,909	255,194	98,716	111,889	92,053	19,837
1976	540,120	379,950	265,589	114,361	160,170	132,141	28,029
1977	516,612	363,725	254,473	109,253	152,887	128,014	24,873
1978	536,385	364,987	230,691	134,296	171,398	148,203	23,195
1979	601,486	425,934	283,667	142,267	175,552	143,306	32,246
1980	642,654	472,639	321,602	151,037	170,015	137,467	32,547
1981	636,547	485,653	338,693	146,960	150,894	115,439	35,455
1982	602,246	457,696	309,453	148,243	144,550	111,058	33,492
1983	653,690	501,124	309,364	191,760	152,566	123,885	28,681
1984	694,803	519,902	316,132	203,770	174,901	135,158	39,743
1985	653,593	500,876	293,614	207,262	152,717	120,190	32,527
1986	700,115	537,361	308,187	229,174	162,754	124,828	37,927
1987	682,283	531,904	295,906	235,997	150,380	110,243	40,136
1988	677,134	512,215	285,013	227,201	164,920	122,718	42,202
1989	619,712	494,351	254,234	240,117	125,361	102,870	22,491
1990	713,135	542,233	309,971	232,262	170,903	126,117	44,785
1991	716,291	567,682	314,108	253,574	148,610	129,738	18,872
1992	819,616	645,538	370,610	274,928	174,079	125,818	48,261
1993	745,962	593,449	341,191	252,258	152,513	119,763	32,750
1994	820,025	659,307	391,561	267,746	160,718	119,430	41,289
1995	848,299	697,501	415,503	281,998	150,798	112,401	38,397
1996	877,906	724,686	424,979	299,707	153,220	113,435	39,785
1997	955,359	764,906	462,596	302,310	190,453	138,411	52,041
1998	997,263	806,981	486,340	320,641	190,282	147,697	42,585
1999	836,776	640,679	417,631	223,048	196,096	147,803	48,293
2000	770,487	583,740	366,883	216,857	186,747	141,839	44,908
2001	730,689	557,774	367,964	189,810	172,915	124,915	47,999
2002	791,811	584,014	405,884	178,130	207,797	146,864	60,933
2003	675,698	521,098	342,360	178,737	154,600	114,134	40,466
2004	732,691	556,824	383,446	173,378	175,867	140,327	35,541
2005	730,484	562,783	372,736	190,046	167,701	130,443	37,258
2006	747,860	574,013	384,515	189,498	173,847	137,077	36,770

Table A.6a—Trends in pulpwood production by species group, Arkansas, 1953 to 2006

Year	Total production	Roundwood			Residues		
		Total	Softwood	Hardwood	Total	Softwood	Hardwood
				standard cords			
1953	784,644	780,982	673,241	107,741	3,662	1,322	2,340
1954	832,679	826,272	725,620	100,652	6,407	4,355	2,052
1955	895,213	876,999	782,715	94,284	18,214	12,608	5,606
1956	1,075,233	934,734	802,358	132,376	140,499	133,159	7,340
1957	1,042,386	832,198	709,887	122,311	210,188	206,207	3,981
1958	1,314,356	1,041,463	893,548	147,915	272,893	264,945	7,948
1959	1,524,266	1,192,363	1,001,946	190,417	331,903	323,451	8,452
1960	1,555,921	1,216,360	983,258	233,102	339,561	329,494	10,067
1961	1,642,825	1,235,828	987,044	248,784	406,997	385,769	21,228
1962	1,729,836	1,310,029	974,038	335,991	419,807	407,404	12,403
1963	1,850,373	1,372,070	1,003,058	369,012	478,303	461,198	17,105
1964	2,062,407	1,497,319	1,041,729	455,590	565,088	548,684	16,404
1965	2,092,244	1,511,136	968,929	542,207	581,108	563,014	18,094
1966	2,193,153	1,544,752	989,866	554,886	648,401	614,684	33,717
1967	2,208,405	1,458,877	1,021,611	437,266	749,528	679,604	69,924
1968	2,297,638	1,532,142	1,011,888	520,254	765,496	659,314	106,182
1969	2,578,998	1,743,003	1,121,784	621,219	835,995	688,615	147,380
1970	2,574,196	1,667,590	1,122,937	544,653	906,606	733,787	172,819
1971	3,175,448	1,884,564	1,236,179	648,385	1,290,884	1,130,716	160,168
1972	3,393,913	2,132,138	1,343,265	788,873	1,261,775	1,113,871	147,904
1973	3,375,595	1,957,719	1,255,288	702,431	1,417,876	1,269,172	148,704
1974	3,291,137	2,139,013	1,402,177	736,836	1,152,124	986,713	165,411
1975	3,242,472	1,983,759	1,360,210	623,549	1,258,713	1,105,521	153,192
1976	3,533,082	2,294,172	1,482,333	811,839	1,238,910	1,111,427	127,483
1977	3,498,639	2,220,196	1,454,603	765,593	1,278,443	1,118,424	160,019
1978	3,948,024	2,332,426	1,447,372	885,054	1,615,598	1,373,322	242,276
1979	4,069,147	2,500,836	1,596,876	903,960	1,568,311	1,269,214	299,097
1980	4,321,529	2,259,582	1,498,250	761,332	2,061,947	1,578,244	483,696
1981	4,232,057	1,992,860	1,366,182	626,678	2,239,197	1,658,778	580,419
1982	4,146,201	1,933,810	1,220,643	713,167	2,212,391	1,619,788	592,603
1983	4,172,315	1,809,905	1,061,851	748,054	2,362,410	1,837,218	525,192
1984	4,339,929	1,578,389	949,936	628,452	2,761,540	2,017,519	744,021
1985	4,130,838	1,637,898	847,690	790,208	2,492,940	1,851,318	641,622
1986	4,477,922	1,766,185	871,779	894,406	2,711,737	1,960,824	750,913
1987	5,013,260	2,070,667	1,154,024	916,643	2,942,593	2,108,006	834,587
1988	5,007,894	2,333,448	1,169,028	1,164,420	2,674,446	1,870,819	803,627
1989	4,861,947	2,306,544	1,340,899	965,645	2,555,403	1,713,391	842,012
1990	4,985,939	2,634,899	1,675,840	959,059	2,351,040	1,483,806	867,234
1991	4,638,928	2,547,734	1,538,744	1,008,990	2,091,194	1,391,280	699,914
1992	4,816,728	2,213,335	1,387,127	826,208	2,603,393	1,723,597	879,796
1993	4,607,099	2,021,805	1,164,206	857,599	2,585,294	1,746,887	838,407
1994	4,260,794	1,986,589	1,251,380	735,209	2,274,205	1,561,002	713,203
1995	4,479,901	2,733,456	1,387,611	1,345,845	1,746,445	1,397,460	348,985
1996	4,652,494	3,186,346	1,664,650	1,521,696	1,466,148	1,325,715	140,433
1997	4,749,149	3,068,329	1,751,737	1,316,592	1,680,820	1,297,795	383,025
1998	4,678,729	3,252,980	2,002,113	1,250,867	1,425,749	1,282,048	143,701
1999	6,296,225	3,788,619	2,464,337	1,324,282	2,507,606	2,039,866	467,740
2000	4,937,547	2,928,431	1,902,073	1,026,358	2,009,116	1,758,352	250,764
2001	4,537,977	2,767,238	1,656,253	1,110,985	1,770,739	1,511,177	259,562
2002	4,617,788	2,821,679	1,807,590	1,014,089	1,796,109	1,438,097	358,012
2003	4,407,608	2,832,098	1,784,684	1,047,414	1,575,510	1,340,821	234,689
2004	4,790,314	3,331,705	1,945,578	1,386,127	1,458,609	1,340,546	118,063
2005	4,617,883	3,117,078	1,767,009	1,350,069	1,500,805	1,366,573	134,232
2006	4,571,894	3,090,861	1,785,073	1,305,788	1,481,033	1,322,110	158,923

Table A.6b—Trends in pulpwood production by species group, Arkansas, 1953 to 2006

Year	Total production	Roundwood Total	Roundwood Softwood	Roundwood Hardwood	Residues Total	Residues Softwood	Residues Hardwood
				green tons			
1953	2,128,373	2,119,426	1,817,751	301,675	8,948	3,179	5,768
1954	2,256,532	2,241,000	1,959,174	281,826	15,532	10,474	5,058
1955	2,421,467	2,377,326	2,113,331	263,995	44,141	30,322	13,819
1956	2,875,360	2,537,019	2,166,367	370,653	338,340	320,247	18,093
1957	2,764,907	2,259,166	1,916,695	342,471	505,741	495,928	9,813
1958	3,483,526	2,826,742	2,412,580	414,162	656,785	637,193	19,592
1959	4,037,156	3,238,422	2,705,254	533,168	798,734	777,900	20,834
1960	4,124,730	3,307,482	2,654,797	652,686	817,248	792,433	24,815
1961	4,341,715	3,361,614	2,665,019	696,595	980,101	927,774	52,327
1962	4,581,057	3,570,677	2,629,903	940,775	1,010,380	979,807	30,573
1963	4,892,835	3,741,490	2,708,257	1,033,234	1,151,345	1,109,181	42,164
1964	5,448,341	4,088,320	2,812,668	1,275,652	1,360,021	1,319,585	40,436
1965	5,532,938	4,134,288	2,616,108	1,518,180	1,398,650	1,354,049	44,602
1966	5,787,746	4,226,319	2,672,638	1,553,681	1,561,427	1,478,315	83,112
1967	5,789,505	3,982,695	2,758,350	1,224,345	1,806,810	1,634,448	172,363
1968	6,036,198	4,188,809	2,732,098	1,456,711	1,847,389	1,585,650	261,739
1969	6,787,641	4,768,230	3,028,817	1,739,413	2,019,411	1,656,119	363,292
1970	6,747,715	4,556,958	3,031,930	1,525,028	2,190,757	1,764,758	425,999
1971	8,267,347	5,153,161	3,337,683	1,815,478	3,114,186	2,719,372	394,814
1972	8,879,103	5,835,660	3,626,816	2,208,844	3,043,443	2,678,860	364,583
1973	8,774,998	5,356,084	3,389,278	1,966,807	3,418,914	3,052,359	366,555
1974	8,629,802	5,849,019	3,785,878	2,063,141	2,780,783	2,373,045	407,738
1975	8,454,900	5,418,504	3,672,567	1,745,937	3,036,396	2,658,778	377,618
1976	9,262,676	6,275,448	4,002,299	2,273,149	2,987,228	2,672,982	314,246
1977	9,155,345	6,071,089	3,927,428	2,143,660	3,084,257	2,689,810	394,447
1978	10,286,105	6,386,056	3,907,904	2,478,151	3,900,050	3,302,839	597,210
1979	10,632,387	6,842,653	4,311,565	2,531,088	3,789,734	3,052,460	737,274
1980	11,164,992	6,177,005	4,045,275	2,131,730	4,987,987	3,795,677	1,192,311
1981	10,863,484	5,443,390	3,688,691	1,754,698	5,420,094	3,989,361	1,430,733
1982	10,648,960	5,292,604	3,295,736	1,996,868	5,356,357	3,895,590	1,460,766
1983	10,674,656	4,961,549	2,866,998	2,094,551	5,713,108	4,418,509	1,294,598
1984	11,010,638	4,324,493	2,564,827	1,759,666	6,686,145	4,852,133	1,834,012
1985	10,535,363	4,501,345	2,288,763	2,212,582	6,034,018	4,452,420	1,581,598
1986	11,424,922	4,858,140	2,353,803	2,504,337	6,566,782	4,715,782	1,851,001
1987	12,809,477	5,682,465	3,115,865	2,566,600	7,127,011	5,069,754	2,057,257
1988	12,897,012	6,416,752	3,156,376	3,260,376	6,480,260	4,499,320	1,980,941
1989	12,520,498	6,324,233	3,620,427	2,703,806	6,196,265	4,120,705	2,075,560
1990	12,916,418	7,210,133	4,524,768	2,685,365	5,706,285	3,568,553	2,137,732
1991	12,051,097	6,979,781	4,154,609	2,825,172	5,071,316	3,346,028	1,725,288
1992	12,372,573	6,058,625	3,745,243	2,313,382	6,313,948	4,145,251	2,168,697
1993	11,812,570	5,544,633	3,143,356	2,401,277	6,267,936	4,201,263	2,066,673
1994	10,949,566	5,437,311	3,378,726	2,058,585	5,512,255	3,754,210	1,758,045
1995	11,736,055	7,514,916	3,746,550	3,768,366	4,221,139	3,360,891	860,248
1996	12,289,816	8,755,304	4,494,555	4,260,749	3,534,512	3,188,345	346,167
1997	12,481,501	8,416,148	4,729,690	3,686,458	4,065,354	3,121,197	944,157
1998	12,345,681	8,908,133	5,405,705	3,502,428	3,437,548	3,083,325	354,223
1999	16,420,556	10,361,700	6,653,710	3,707,990	6,058,857	4,905,878	1,152,979
2000	12,856,369	8,009,400	5,135,597	2,873,802	4,846,970	4,228,837	618,133
2001	11,856,842	7,582,641	4,471,883	3,110,758	4,274,201	3,634,381	639,820
2002	12,061,065	7,719,942	4,880,493	2,839,449	4,341,123	3,458,623	882,500
2003	11,554,589	7,751,406	4,818,647	2,932,759	3,803,183	3,224,675	578,508
2004	12,649,255	9,134,216	5,253,061	3,881,156	3,515,038	3,224,013	291,025
2005	12,168,607	8,551,118	4,770,924	3,780,193	3,617,490	3,286,608	330,882
2006	12,047,323	8,475,904	4,819,697	3,656,206	3,571,420	3,179,675	391,745

Table A.6c—Trends in pulpwood production by species group, Arkansas, 1953 to 2006

Year	Total production	Roundwood			Residues		
		Total	Softwood	Hardwood	Total	Softwood	Hardwood
				thousand cubic feet			
1953	59,146	58,897	50,493	8,404	249	88	161
1954	62,704	62,272	54,421	7,851	432	291	141
1955	67,285	66,057	58,704	7,354	1,227	842	385
1956	79,902	70,502	60,177	10,325	9,400	8,896	504
1957	76,830	62,781	53,241	9,540	14,049	13,776	273
1958	96,799	78,553	67,016	11,537	18,246	17,700	546
1959	120,323	96,391	81,158	15,233	23,932	23,337	595
1960	122,774	98,292	79,644	18,648	24,482	23,773	709
1961	129,182	99,853	79,951	19,903	29,328	27,833	1,495
1962	136,044	105,776	78,897	26,879	30,268	29,394	874
1963	145,249	110,769	81,248	29,521	34,480	33,276	1,205
1964	161,570	120,827	84,380	36,447	40,743	39,588	1,155
1965	163,756	121,860	78,483	43,377	41,896	40,622	1,274
1966	171,294	124,570	80,179	44,391	46,724	44,350	2,375
1967	171,690	117,732	82,750	34,981	53,958	49,034	4,925
1968	178,631	123,583	81,963	41,620	55,048	47,570	7,478
1969	200,626	140,562	90,865	49,698	60,064	49,684	10,380
1970	199,644	134,530	90,958	43,572	65,114	52,943	12,171
1971	244,863	152,001	100,130	51,871	92,862	81,581	11,280
1972	262,697	171,914	108,804	63,110	90,783	80,366	10,417
1973	259,917	157,873	101,678	56,194	102,044	91,571	10,473
1974	255,365	172,523	113,576	58,947	82,841	71,192	11,650
1975	250,614	160,061	110,177	49,884	90,553	79,764	10,789
1976	274,184	185,016	120,069	64,947	89,168	80,190	8,978
1977	271,035	179,070	117,823	61,247	91,965	80,695	11,270
1978	304,190	188,041	117,237	70,804	116,149	99,086	17,063
1979	314,303	201,664	129,347	72,317	112,639	91,574	21,065
1980	330,202	182,265	121,358	60,907	147,937	113,871	34,066
1981	321,354	160,795	110,661	50,134	160,559	119,681	40,878
1982	314,530	155,925	98,872	57,053	158,604	116,868	41,736
1983	315,399	145,854	86,010	59,844	169,544	132,556	36,989
1984	325,186	127,221	76,945	50,276	197,965	145,565	52,400
1985	310,641	131,880	68,663	63,217	178,762	133,573	45,189
1986	336,526	142,167	70,614	71,552	194,360	141,474	52,886
1987	377,673	166,801	93,474	73,327	210,872	152,093	58,779
1988	357,249	177,917	87,093	90,825	179,331	124,148	55,183
1989	346,737	175,217	99,897	75,320	171,520	113,701	57,819
1990	357,673	199,657	124,850	74,807	158,017	98,466	59,551
1991	333,725	193,338	114,636	78,701	140,387	92,326	48,062
1992	342,577	167,785	103,341	64,444	174,792	114,378	60,414
1993	327,121	153,626	86,733	66,893	173,495	115,924	57,572
1994	303,137	150,574	93,228	57,346	152,563	103,588	48,974
1995	325,053	208,353	103,377	104,976	116,700	92,736	23,964
1996	340,033	242,475	125,131	117,344	97,558	88,021	9,537
1997	345,384	233,204	131,676	101,528	112,180	86,167	26,013
1998	341,837	246,956	150,497	96,459	94,881	85,122	9,759
1999	452,168	284,965	182,819	102,146	167,203	135,437	31,766
2000	354,050	220,273	141,107	79,166	133,776	116,746	17,030
2001	326,527	208,564	122,871	85,694	117,963	100,335	17,628
2002	332,389	212,593	134,317	78,276	119,797	95,483	24,314
2003	318,426	213,463	132,615	80,849	104,963	89,024	15,939
2004	348,588	251,564	144,570	106,994	97,024	89,006	8,018
2005	333,800	234,622	130,774	103,848	99,178	90,088	9,090
2006	330,472	232,553	132,111	100,441	97,919	87,157	10,762

Table A.7a—Trends in pulpwood production by species group, Florida, 1953 to 2006

Year	Total production	Roundwood			Residues		
		Total	Softwood	Hardwood	Total	Softwood	Hardwood
				standard cords			
1953	1,682,742	1,674,864	1,671,156	3,708	7,878	2,844	5,034
1954	1,674,502	1,661,617	1,661,202	415	12,885	8,758	4,127
1955	1,866,516	1,828,541	1,826,962	1,579	37,975	26,286	11,689
1956	1,959,699	1,950,653	1,949,912	741	9,046	3,823	5,223
1957	1,997,493	1,947,379	1,921,422	25,957	50,114	48,933	1,181
1958	1,834,883	1,752,278	1,690,760	61,518	82,605	79,287	3,318
1959	2,113,421	1,979,341	1,882,574	96,767	134,080	123,191	10,889
1960	2,100,426	1,923,892	1,825,216	98,676	176,534	164,006	12,528
1961	2,265,429	2,058,749	1,954,389	104,360	206,680	180,974	25,706
1962	2,464,414	2,252,576	2,111,499	141,077	211,838	174,361	37,477
1963	2,527,962	2,289,060	2,121,628	167,432	238,902	194,902	44,000
1964	2,745,195	2,482,429	2,238,859	243,570	262,766	217,477	45,289
1965	2,874,377	2,597,269	2,324,844	272,425	277,108	226,580	50,528
1966	2,989,962	2,676,156	2,424,176	251,980	313,806	254,802	59,004
1967	2,925,592	2,588,722	2,352,273	236,449	336,870	252,879	83,991
1968	3,243,503	2,808,606	2,511,959	296,647	434,897	344,678	90,219
1969	3,446,032	3,020,675	2,752,235	268,440	425,357	330,271	95,086
1970	3,425,210	2,941,938	2,708,191	233,747	483,272	391,006	92,266
1971	3,374,788	2,886,491	2,662,041	224,450	488,297	400,968	87,329
1972	3,393,398	2,896,159	2,687,235	208,924	497,239	397,623	99,616
1973	3,491,408	3,010,011	2,783,124	226,887	481,397	396,421	84,976
1974	3,377,046	2,889,076	2,654,794	234,282	487,970	367,284	120,686
1975	2,991,423	2,534,698	2,320,420	214,278	456,725	337,713	119,012
1976	3,304,192	2,667,591	2,412,376	255,215	636,601	522,209	114,392
1977	3,630,252	2,799,352	2,513,674	285,678	830,900	723,979	106,921
1978	3,670,765	2,925,063	2,595,172	329,891	745,702	653,211	92,491
1979	3,832,971	3,042,860	2,698,019	344,841	790,111	699,414	90,697
1980	3,829,647	3,012,848	2,701,519	311,329	816,799	698,820	117,979
1981	4,057,439	3,113,732	2,774,549	339,183	943,707	775,691	168,016
1982	3,962,786	3,089,274	2,779,482	309,792	873,512	785,491	88,021
1983	4,376,931	3,262,214	2,913,976	348,238	1,114,717	1,031,804	82,913
1984	4,434,133	3,100,007	2,834,541	265,466	1,334,126	1,242,712	91,414
1985	3,946,024	2,781,001	2,551,665	229,336	1,165,023	1,136,927	28,096
1986	4,109,725	3,039,883	2,823,761	216,122	1,069,842	1,025,631	44,211
1987	4,645,511	3,529,888	3,260,971	268,917	1,115,623	1,086,330	29,293
1988	4,896,849	3,803,299	3,415,647	387,652	1,093,550	1,055,231	38,319
1989	5,095,094	3,788,983	3,464,688	324,295	1,306,111	1,097,292	208,819
1990	5,016,740	4,001,129	3,602,040	399,089	1,015,611	884,293	131,318
1991	4,907,015	4,191,655	3,815,133	376,522	715,360	665,773	49,587
1992	4,935,158	4,268,859	3,851,608	417,251	666,299	617,179	49,120
1993	4,679,754	3,904,051	3,394,989	509,062	775,703	736,291	39,412
1994	4,744,716	3,862,962	3,409,787	453,175	881,754	854,611	27,143
1995	5,287,491	4,407,124	3,874,486	532,638	880,367	863,534	16,833
1996	4,703,887	3,922,617	3,516,924	405,693	781,270	769,618	11,652
1997	4,659,798	3,911,831	3,435,336	476,495	747,967	733,405	14,562
1998	4,821,365	3,985,054	3,517,097	467,957	836,311	823,492	12,819
1999	4,267,655	3,551,622	3,030,634	520,988	716,033	706,731	9,302
2000	4,427,197	3,610,970	3,091,647	519,323	816,227	771,861	44,366
2001	4,469,415	3,540,786	2,948,147	592,639	928,629	899,261	29,368
2002	4,451,531	3,464,350	3,032,006	432,344	987,181	882,363	104,818
2003	4,617,315	3,725,983	3,368,490	357,493	891,332	883,564	7,768
2004	4,629,538	3,415,777	3,140,075	275,702	1,213,761	1,159,056	54,705
2005	4,188,856	2,934,707	2,668,248	266,459	1,254,149	1,197,702	56,447
2006	4,279,351	3,082,224	2,847,401	234,823	1,197,127	1,162,115	35,012

Table A.7b—Trends in pulpwood production by species group, Florida, 1953 to 2006

Year	Total production	Roundwood			Residues		
		Total	Softwood	Hardwood	Total	Softwood	Hardwood
				green tons			
1953	4,541,752	4,522,504	4,512,121	10,382	19,249	6,840	12,409
1954	4,517,643	4,486,407	4,485,245	1,162	31,236	21,063	10,173
1955	5,029,250	4,937,219	4,932,797	4,421	92,031	63,218	28,813
1956	5,288,906	5,266,837	5,264,762	2,075	22,069	9,194	12,875
1957	5,381,114	5,260,519	5,187,839	72,680	120,595	117,684	2,911
1958	4,936,167	4,737,302	4,565,052	172,250	198,864	190,685	8,179
1959	5,677,013	5,353,897	5,082,950	270,948	323,116	296,274	26,841
1960	5,629,692	5,204,376	4,928,083	276,293	425,316	394,434	30,882
1961	6,067,666	5,569,058	5,276,850	292,208	498,608	435,242	63,365
1962	6,607,782	6,096,063	5,701,047	395,016	511,719	419,338	92,381
1963	6,774,405	6,197,205	5,728,396	468,810	577,199	468,739	108,460
1964	7,361,585	6,726,915	6,044,919	681,996	634,670	523,032	111,637
1965	7,709,345	7,039,869	6,277,079	762,790	669,476	544,925	124,552
1966	8,009,063	7,250,819	6,545,275	705,544	758,244	612,799	145,445
1967	7,828,406	7,013,194	6,351,137	662,057	815,212	608,174	207,038
1968	8,664,241	7,612,901	6,782,289	830,612	1,051,340	828,951	222,390
1969	9,211,355	8,182,667	7,431,035	751,632	1,028,689	794,302	234,387
1970	9,134,412	7,966,607	7,312,116	654,492	1,167,805	940,369	227,436
1971	8,995,565	7,815,971	7,187,511	628,460	1,179,594	964,328	215,266
1972	9,042,358	7,840,522	7,255,535	584,987	1,201,837	956,283	245,553
1973	9,312,577	8,149,718	7,514,435	635,284	1,162,858	953,393	209,466
1974	9,004,742	7,823,933	7,167,944	655,990	1,180,809	883,318	297,491
1975	7,970,677	6,865,112	6,265,134	599,978	1,105,564	812,200	293,365
1976	8,765,906	7,228,017	6,513,415	714,602	1,537,889	1,255,913	281,976
1977	9,591,548	7,586,818	6,786,920	799,898	2,004,730	1,741,169	263,560
1978	9,729,622	7,930,659	7,006,964	923,695	1,798,963	1,570,972	227,990
1979	10,155,865	8,250,206	7,284,651	965,555	1,905,659	1,682,091	223,568
1980	10,137,303	8,165,823	7,294,101	871,721	1,971,480	1,680,662	290,818
1981	10,720,691	8,440,995	7,491,282	949,712	2,279,696	1,865,537	414,159
1982	10,478,097	8,372,019	7,504,601	867,418	2,106,078	1,889,106	216,972
1983	11,528,671	8,842,802	7,867,735	975,066	2,685,869	2,481,489	204,381
1984	11,610,623	8,396,566	7,653,261	743,305	3,214,058	2,988,722	225,336
1985	10,335,202	7,531,636	6,889,496	642,141	2,803,566	2,734,309	69,257
1986	10,804,919	8,229,296	7,624,155	605,142	2,575,623	2,466,643	108,980
1987	12,242,420	9,557,589	8,804,622	752,968	2,684,831	2,612,624	72,207
1988	12,939,959	10,307,673	9,222,247	1,085,426	2,632,287	2,537,831	94,456
1989	13,416,410	10,262,684	9,354,658	908,026	3,153,726	2,638,987	514,739
1990	13,293,381	10,842,957	9,725,508	1,117,449	2,450,424	2,126,725	323,699
1991	13,078,537	11,355,121	10,300,859	1,054,262	1,723,416	1,601,184	122,232
1992	13,173,041	11,567,644	10,399,342	1,168,303	1,605,396	1,484,315	121,081
1993	12,459,774	10,591,844	9,166,470	1,425,374	1,867,930	1,770,780	97,151
1994	12,597,562	10,475,315	9,206,425	1,268,890	2,122,247	2,055,339	66,907
1995	14,070,791	11,952,499	10,461,112	1,491,386	2,118,293	2,076,799	41,493
1996	12,511,289	10,631,635	9,495,695	1,135,940	1,879,653	1,850,931	28,722
1997	12,409,328	10,609,593	9,275,407	1,334,186	1,799,734	1,763,839	35,895
1998	12,818,539	10,806,442	9,496,162	1,310,280	2,012,097	1,980,498	31,599
1999	11,364,096	9,641,478	8,182,712	1,458,766	1,722,617	1,699,688	22,929
2000	11,767,239	9,801,551	8,347,447	1,454,104	1,965,688	1,856,326	109,362
2001	11,854,501	9,619,386	7,959,997	1,659,389	2,235,115	2,162,723	72,392
2002	11,777,439	9,396,979	8,186,416	1,210,563	2,380,459	2,122,083	258,376
2003	12,240,023	10,095,903	9,094,923	1,000,980	2,144,120	2,124,971	19,148
2004	12,172,546	9,250,168	8,478,203	771,966	2,922,378	2,787,530	134,848
2005	10,969,970	7,950,355	7,204,270	746,085	3,019,615	2,880,473	139,142
2006	11,226,678	8,345,487	7,687,983	657,504	2,881,191	2,794,887	86,305

Table A.7c—Trends in pulpwood production by species group, Florida, 1953 to 2006

Year	Total production	Roundwood Total	Softwood	Hardwood	Residues Total	Softwood	Hardwood
				thousand cubic feet			
1953	133,536	132,983	132,688	294	553	201	352
1954	132,839	131,931	131,898	33	908	619	289
1955	147,861	145,185	145,059	125	2,676	1,859	817
1956	155,516	154,880	154,821	59	636	270	365
1957	158,164	154,621	152,559	2,061	3,543	3,461	83
1958	144,969	139,130	134,245	4,885	5,839	5,608	232
1959	150,538	141,962	134,792	7,171	8,575	7,872	703
1960	149,286	137,997	130,685	7,312	11,289	10,480	809
1961	160,891	147,667	139,934	7,733	13,224	11,565	1,660
1962	175,198	161,637	151,183	10,454	13,562	11,142	2,420
1963	179,610	164,315	151,908	12,407	15,296	12,455	2,841
1964	195,172	178,350	160,302	18,049	16,821	13,897	2,924
1965	204,386	186,645	166,458	20,187	17,741	14,479	3,262
1966	212,334	192,242	173,570	18,672	20,092	16,283	3,809
1967	207,526	185,943	168,422	17,521	21,582	16,160	5,423
1968	229,688	201,837	179,856	21,982	27,851	22,026	5,825
1969	245,999	218,755	200,528	18,227	27,244	21,105	6,139
1970	245,815	213,298	197,427	15,871	32,516	26,389	6,128
1971	242,163	209,303	194,063	15,240	32,861	27,061	5,800
1972	243,536	210,085	195,899	14,186	33,451	26,835	6,616
1973	250,651	218,254	202,863	15,391	32,398	26,754	5,644
1974	242,204	209,401	193,509	15,893	32,803	24,788	8,015
1975	214,358	183,662	169,131	14,531	30,696	22,792	7,904
1976	240,115	197,274	175,834	21,441	42,840	35,243	7,597
1977	284,631	228,669	204,669	24,000	55,962	48,861	7,101
1978	289,246	239,019	211,305	27,714	50,227	44,084	6,143
1979	309,849	256,623	227,903	28,720	53,226	47,203	6,023
1980	328,680	266,206	239,777	26,429	62,475	53,843	8,632
1981	347,111	275,052	246,259	28,793	72,059	59,766	12,293
1982	339,956	272,995	246,697	26,298	66,961	60,521	6,440
1983	365,416	279,851	251,211	28,640	85,565	79,499	6,066
1984	364,342	261,905	240,224	21,681	102,437	95,749	6,688
1985	323,791	234,137	215,584	18,553	89,654	87,598	2,056
1986	336,258	254,000	236,560	17,440	82,258	79,023	3,235
1987	366,841	288,470	267,032	21,438	78,371	76,291	2,080
1988	387,429	310,602	279,698	30,904	76,828	74,107	2,720
1989	388,199	296,313	270,713	25,600	91,886	77,061	14,825
1990	384,374	312,949	281,445	31,504	71,425	62,102	9,323
1991	379,667	329,390	298,454	30,936	50,277	46,756	3,520
1992	382,421	335,590	301,307	34,282	46,831	43,343	3,487
1993	358,262	303,756	262,372	41,384	54,507	51,709	2,798
1994	362,301	300,356	263,515	36,841	61,945	60,018	1,927
1995	378,170	321,011	280,917	40,094	57,159	56,043	1,116
1996	336,251	285,530	254,992	30,538	50,720	49,948	772
1997	336,064	287,501	251,618	35,883	48,563	47,598	965
1998	347,140	292,847	257,607	35,240	54,294	53,444	850
1999	307,804	261,321	222,119	39,202	46,483	45,866	617
2000	318,702	265,668	226,591	39,077	53,034	50,093	2,941
2001	320,975	260,667	216,074	44,593	60,308	58,361	1,947
2002	318,965	254,752	222,220	32,532	64,213	57,265	6,948
2003	328,593	270,735	243,796	26,939	57,858	57,343	515
2004	326,888	248,040	227,264	20,776	78,848	75,222	3,626
2005	294,973	213,501	193,390	20,111	81,472	77,730	3,742
2006	301,840	224,098	206,375	17,723	77,741	75,421	2,321

Table A.8a—Trends in pulpwood production by species group, Georgia, 1953 to 2006

Year	Total production	Roundwood			Residues		
		Total	Softwood	Hardwood	Total	Softwood	Hardwood
				standard cords			
1953	2,892,710	2,879,168	2,748,853	130,315	13,542	4,890	8,652
1954	3,081,187	3,057,478	2,879,901	177,577	23,709	16,116	7,593
1955	3,837,619	3,759,540	3,568,766	190,774	78,079	54,046	24,033
1956	3,888,601	3,849,942	3,665,084	184,858	38,659	20,452	18,207
1957	3,859,010	3,773,376	3,543,348	230,028	85,634	70,375	15,259
1958	4,092,917	3,860,449	3,583,457	276,992	232,468	211,622	20,846
1959	4,735,090	4,354,499	4,009,054	345,445	380,591	353,644	26,947
1960	4,905,838	4,410,128	4,004,707	405,421	495,710	439,728	55,982
1961	4,949,086	4,406,010	3,923,858	482,152	543,076	463,663	79,413
1962	5,216,995	4,556,284	4,057,491	498,793	660,711	559,901	100,810
1963	5,520,415	4,800,709	4,269,843	530,866	719,706	621,803	97,903
1964	5,842,876	5,082,173	4,556,129	526,044	760,703	652,912	107,791
1965	6,159,581	5,346,821	4,776,537	570,284	812,760	689,057	123,703
1966	6,298,107	5,426,502	4,865,959	560,543	871,605	726,513	145,092
1967	6,326,341	5,425,783	4,840,402	585,381	900,558	736,572	163,986
1968	6,919,245	5,792,145	5,108,656	683,489	1,127,100	967,099	160,001
1969	7,303,511	6,108,468	5,385,377	723,091	1,195,043	1,013,426	181,617
1970	7,280,532	6,178,238	5,584,797	593,441	1,102,294	916,279	186,015
1971	7,258,118	5,720,910	5,116,574	604,336	1,537,208	1,314,522	222,686
1972	7,565,077	6,003,561	5,316,989	686,572	1,561,516	1,346,487	215,029
1973	7,866,244	6,092,065	5,444,199	647,866	1,774,179	1,524,493	249,686
1974	8,117,780	6,210,712	5,517,091	693,621	1,907,068	1,576,092	330,976
1975	6,957,206	5,179,111	4,578,469	600,642	1,778,095	1,549,087	229,008
1976	7,773,719	5,599,243	4,965,781	633,462	2,174,476	1,909,786	264,690
1977	8,365,444	5,830,272	5,133,149	697,123	2,535,172	2,244,386	290,786
1978	8,908,243	6,057,772	5,303,463	754,309	2,850,471	2,493,985	356,486
1979	9,257,694	6,205,383	5,505,965	699,418	3,052,311	2,628,614	423,697
1980	8,812,454	6,001,253	5,392,473	608,780	2,811,201	2,425,614	385,587
1981	8,866,761	6,143,155	5,394,174	748,981	2,723,606	2,349,386	374,220
1982	8,745,095	6,125,794	5,304,281	821,513	2,619,301	2,320,389	298,912
1983	9,590,017	6,374,806	5,479,927	894,879	3,215,211	2,834,816	380,395
1984	9,815,466	6,434,870	5,516,215	918,655	3,380,596	2,928,698	451,898
1985	9,838,850	6,529,334	5,443,448	1,085,886	3,309,516	2,957,031	352,485
1986	10,212,843	7,125,514	5,883,737	1,241,777	3,087,329	2,818,906	268,423
1987	10,659,329	7,322,797	6,075,372	1,247,425	3,336,532	3,066,424	270,108
1988	9,880,290	6,634,149	5,245,909	1,388,240	3,246,141	2,972,517	273,624
1989	8,950,857	6,225,757	4,857,841	1,367,916	2,725,100	2,576,889	148,211
1990	9,293,585	6,541,070	5,252,415	1,288,655	2,752,515	2,602,687	149,828
1991	9,756,638	7,119,835	5,608,114	1,511,721	2,636,803	2,284,986	351,817
1992	10,225,455	7,040,941	5,503,551	1,537,390	3,184,514	2,738,996	445,518
1993	9,635,900	7,004,262	5,067,648	1,936,614	2,631,638	2,339,522	292,116
1994	9,616,509	6,898,119	5,076,886	1,821,233	2,718,390	2,396,399	321,991
1995	11,147,878	8,019,206	5,503,023	2,516,183	3,128,672	2,498,099	630,573
1996	10,003,071	7,373,429	5,320,805	2,052,624	2,629,642	2,349,151	280,491
1997	11,390,306	8,051,665	5,723,950	2,327,715	3,338,641	2,417,776	920,865
1998	10,249,549	7,109,288	5,124,636	1,984,652	3,140,261	2,310,969	829,292
1999	10,702,207	7,886,313	5,751,625	2,134,688	2,815,894	2,206,692	609,202
2000	10,294,982	7,493,733	5,497,173	1,996,560	2,801,249	2,170,847	630,402
2001	9,964,863	6,681,892	4,915,186	1,766,706	3,282,971	2,416,057	866,914
2002	9,924,035	6,933,528	5,386,913	1,546,615	2,990,507	2,028,116	962,391
2003	9,670,025	7,644,403	6,188,093	1,456,310	2,025,622	1,684,615	341,007
2004	9,890,894	7,571,691	6,428,977	1,142,714	2,319,203	1,800,590	518,613
2005	9,678,133	7,237,990	6,102,607	1,135,383	2,440,143	1,970,639	469,504
2006	10,238,371	7,817,468	6,389,903	1,427,565	2,420,903	1,950,282	470,621

Table A.8b—Trends in pulpwood production by species group, Georgia, 1953 to 2006

Year	Total production	Roundwood			Residues		
		Total	Softwood	Hardwood	Total	Softwood	Hardwood
				green tons			
1953	7,819,873	7,786,785	7,421,903	364,882	33,088	11,760	21,327
1954	8,330,424	8,272,948	7,775,733	497,216	57,476	38,759	18,717
1955	10,359,057	10,169,835	9,635,668	534,167	189,222	129,981	59,241
1956	10,507,397	10,413,329	9,895,727	517,602	94,067	49,187	44,880
1957	10,417,983	10,211,118	9,567,040	644,078	206,865	169,252	37,613
1958	11,011,248	10,450,912	9,675,334	775,578	560,336	508,951	51,385
1959	12,708,630	11,791,692	10,824,446	967,246	916,938	850,514	66,424
1960	13,143,429	11,947,888	10,812,709	1,135,179	1,195,541	1,057,546	137,996
1961	13,255,305	11,944,442	10,594,417	1,350,026	1,310,863	1,115,110	195,753
1962	13,946,905	12,351,846	10,955,226	1,396,620	1,595,059	1,346,562	248,497
1963	14,751,768	13,015,001	11,528,576	1,486,425	1,736,767	1,495,436	241,331
1964	15,610,430	13,774,472	12,301,548	1,472,923	1,835,958	1,570,253	265,705
1965	16,455,555	14,493,445	12,896,650	1,596,795	1,962,110	1,657,182	304,928
1966	16,812,525	14,707,610	13,138,089	1,569,520	2,104,916	1,747,264	357,652
1967	16,883,833	14,708,152	13,069,085	1,639,067	2,175,681	1,771,456	404,225
1968	18,427,416	15,707,140	13,793,371	1,913,769	2,720,276	2,325,873	394,402
1969	19,450,148	16,565,173	14,540,518	2,024,655	2,884,975	2,437,290	447,686
1970	19,402,765	16,740,587	15,078,952	1,661,635	2,662,178	2,203,651	458,527
1971	19,217,237	15,506,891	13,814,750	1,692,141	3,710,346	3,161,425	548,921
1972	20,046,620	16,278,272	14,355,870	1,922,402	3,768,348	3,238,301	530,046
1973	20,795,244	16,513,362	14,699,337	1,814,025	4,281,882	3,666,406	615,476
1974	21,444,642	16,838,285	14,896,146	1,942,139	4,606,357	3,790,501	815,856
1975	18,333,723	14,043,664	12,361,866	1,681,798	4,290,059	3,725,554	564,505
1976	20,426,798	15,181,302	13,407,609	1,773,694	5,245,496	4,593,035	652,461
1977	21,925,983	15,811,447	13,859,502	1,951,944	6,114,536	5,397,748	716,787
1978	23,308,187	16,431,415	14,319,350	2,112,065	6,876,772	5,998,034	878,738
1979	24,190,706	16,824,476	14,866,106	1,958,370	7,366,230	6,321,817	1,044,413
1980	23,048,335	16,264,261	14,559,677	1,704,584	6,784,074	5,833,602	950,472
1981	23,234,142	16,661,417	14,564,270	2,097,147	6,572,726	5,650,273	922,452
1982	22,939,149	16,621,795	14,321,559	2,300,236	6,317,354	5,580,536	736,818
1983	25,056,870	17,301,464	14,795,803	2,505,661	7,755,406	6,817,732	937,674
1984	25,623,462	17,466,015	14,893,781	2,572,234	8,157,447	7,043,519	1,113,929
1985	25,718,325	17,737,790	14,697,310	3,040,481	7,980,535	7,111,660	868,876
1986	26,804,197	19,363,066	15,886,090	3,476,976	7,441,132	6,779,469	661,663
1987	27,936,860	19,896,294	16,403,504	3,492,790	8,040,566	7,374,750	665,816
1988	25,874,413	18,051,026	14,163,954	3,887,072	7,823,387	7,148,903	674,483
1989	23,509,094	16,946,336	13,116,171	3,830,165	6,562,758	6,197,418	365,340
1990	24,418,543	17,789,755	14,181,521	3,608,234	6,628,788	6,259,462	369,326
1991	25,737,347	19,374,727	15,141,908	4,232,819	6,362,620	5,495,391	867,229
1992	26,849,767	19,164,280	14,859,588	4,304,692	7,685,487	6,587,285	1,098,202
1993	25,451,785	19,105,169	13,682,650	5,422,519	6,346,616	5,626,550	720,066
1994	25,364,092	18,807,045	13,707,592	5,099,452	6,557,047	5,763,340	793,708
1995	29,465,765	21,903,475	14,858,162	7,045,312	7,562,291	6,007,928	1,554,362
1996	26,454,639	20,113,521	14,366,174	5,747,347	6,341,118	5,649,708	691,410
1997	30,056,951	21,972,267	15,454,665	6,517,602	8,084,684	5,814,751	2,269,932
1998	26,995,628	19,393,543	13,836,517	5,557,026	7,602,085	5,557,880	2,044,205
1999	28,315,291	21,506,514	15,529,388	5,977,126	6,808,777	5,307,094	1,501,683
2000	27,207,563	20,432,735	14,842,367	5,590,368	6,774,828	5,220,887	1,553,941
2001	26,165,339	18,217,779	13,271,002	4,946,777	7,947,560	5,810,617	2,136,943
2002	26,125,100	18,875,187	14,544,665	4,330,522	7,249,913	4,877,619	2,372,294
2003	25,677,600	20,785,519	16,707,851	4,077,668	4,892,081	4,051,499	840,582
2004	26,166,637	20,557,837	17,358,238	3,199,599	5,608,800	4,330,419	1,278,381
2005	25,552,825	19,656,111	16,477,039	3,179,072	5,896,714	4,739,387	1,157,327
2006	27,100,429	21,249,920	17,252,738	3,997,182	5,850,509	4,690,428	1,160,081

Table A.8c—Trends in pulpwood production by species group, Georgia, 1953 to 2006

Year	Total production	Roundwood			Residues		
		Total	Softwood	Hardwood	Total	Softwood	Hardwood
				thousand cubic feet			
1953	203,221	202,380	193,220	9,160	842	306	535
1954	216,392	214,913	202,431	12,482	1,479	1,009	470
1955	269,133	264,262	250,852	13,410	4,871	3,384	1,487
1956	273,023	270,616	257,622	12,994	2,407	1,281	1,127
1957	270,585	265,234	249,065	16,169	5,351	4,406	944
1958	285,895	271,355	251,885	19,470	14,540	13,250	1,290
1959	329,892	306,082	281,800	24,282	23,810	22,142	1,668
1960	340,988	309,992	281,495	28,497	30,996	27,532	3,464
1961	337,548	302,527	265,844	36,683	35,021	29,655	5,366
1962	355,469	312,847	274,898	37,949	42,622	35,810	6,812
1963	376,059	329,674	289,285	40,389	46,385	39,769	6,615
1964	397,746	348,703	308,681	40,022	49,042	41,759	7,283
1965	419,431	367,002	323,614	43,388	52,429	44,071	8,358
1966	428,590	372,319	329,672	42,647	56,270	46,467	9,804
1967	430,668	372,478	327,941	44,537	58,190	47,110	11,080
1968	523,167	450,502	397,385	53,117	72,665	61,854	10,811
1969	552,194	475,105	418,910	56,195	77,089	64,817	12,272
1970	551,714	480,542	434,422	46,119	71,172	58,604	12,569
1971	544,088	444,967	398,001	46,966	99,121	84,075	15,046
1972	576,794	466,948	413,591	53,357	109,847	94,706	15,141
1973	598,642	473,835	423,486	50,349	124,807	107,226	17,581
1974	620,821	486,661	430,584	56,077	134,160	110,855	23,305
1975	530,970	405,889	357,329	48,560	125,081	108,955	16,125
1976	591,734	438,770	387,557	51,213	152,963	134,325	18,638
1977	613,322	434,987	382,352	52,635	178,335	157,860	20,475
1978	675,412	474,895	413,911	60,983	200,517	175,415	25,102
1979	700,980	486,261	429,716	56,546	214,719	184,884	29,834
1980	703,379	505,622	455,480	50,142	197,757	170,606	27,151
1981	708,909	517,313	455,624	61,690	191,595	165,245	26,350
1982	711,182	515,695	448,031	67,664	195,488	174,536	20,952
1983	780,319	540,426	468,569	71,857	239,894	213,231	26,663
1984	797,405	545,438	471,672	73,766	251,967	220,292	31,675
1985	799,774	552,644	465,450	87,194	247,130	222,423	24,707
1986	819,208	588,360	490,845	97,515	230,848	212,034	18,814
1987	854,375	604,790	506,832	97,959	249,584	230,652	18,933
1988	789,419	546,651	437,635	109,017	242,767	223,588	19,179
1989	709,272	515,863	407,876	107,987	193,409	183,221	10,187
1990	738,089	542,735	441,005	101,730	195,354	185,056	10,298
1991	776,859	590,210	470,871	119,339	186,649	162,467	24,182
1992	773,225	547,855	427,816	120,039	225,370	194,748	30,623
1993	731,564	545,141	393,931	151,210	186,423	166,344	20,079
1994	729,371	536,851	394,649	142,201	192,520	170,388	22,132
1995	838,227	617,265	422,807	194,458	220,962	177,619	43,343
1996	753,748	567,440	408,807	158,633	186,308	167,029	19,280
1997	840,705	617,293	437,957	179,336	223,412	161,344	62,068
1998	755,119	545,007	392,102	152,905	210,112	154,217	55,896
1999	781,871	593,552	431,017	162,535	188,319	147,258	41,061
2000	751,323	563,967	411,949	152,018	187,356	144,866	42,490
2001	720,640	500,979	365,687	135,292	219,661	161,229	58,431
2002	719,429	519,221	400,783	118,438	200,208	135,341	64,867
2003	704,299	568,896	457,619	111,277	135,403	112,418	22,984
2004	717,861	562,747	475,432	87,315	155,113	120,158	34,955
2005	709,337	542,828	455,654	87,174	166,508	134,773	31,735
2006	751,904	586,713	477,105	109,608	165,192	133,381	31,811

Table A.9a—Trends in pulpwood production by species group, Kentucky, 1962 to 2006

Year	Total production	Roundwood Total	Softwood	Hardwood	Residues Total	Softwood	Hardwood
				standard cords			
1953			No data available for 1953 through 1961				
1954							
1955							
1956							
1957							
1958							
1959							
1960							
1961							
1962	82,165	77,165	33,694	43,471	5,000	0	5,000
1963	86,541	80,423	34513	45910	6,118	0	6,118
1964	92,961	84,425	35,804	48,621	8,536	616	7,920
1965	98,940	89,114	36,711	52,403	9,826	706	9,120
1966	154,851	127,434	40,831	86,603	27,417	0	27,417
1967	159,957	86,923	27,906	59,017	73,034	6,923	66,111
1968	177,133	82,919	26,512	56,407	94,214	3,413	90,801
1969	167,960	83,637	27,516	56,121	84,323	6,914	77,409
1970	239,662	115,239	21,625	93,614	124,423	4,722	119,701
1971	304,340	176,311	24,808	151,503	128,029	4,213	123,816
1972	320,155	163,424	24,609	138,815	156,731	5,110	151,621
1973	461,042	230,716	34,014	196,702	230,326	9,321	221,005
1974	396,400	133,100	24,800	108,300	263,300	8,900	254,400
1975	257,551	64,222	12,020	52,202	193,329	6,626	186,703
1976	262,362	62,739	9,721	53,018	199,623	7,018	192,605
1977	278,347	62,823	7,914	54,909	215,524	7,604	207,920
1978	280,344	50,817	6,111	44,706	229,527	4,520	225,007
1979	344,330	60,519	7,719	52,800	283,811	9,101	274,710
1980	354,133	87,720	13,215	74,505	266,413	6,400	260,013
1981	333,943	77,417	11,815	65,602	256,526	2,301	254,225
1982	366,663	103,231	14,414	88,817	263,432	20,409	243,023
1983	522,738	135,632	19,515	116,117	387,106	67,604	319,502
1984	528,331	122,710	14,006	108,704	405,621	25,414	380,207
1985	495,922	128,541	18,068	110,473	367,381	2,396	364,985
1986	380,566	168,568	25,653	142,915	211,998	2,804	209,194
1987	546,598	245,117	34,672	210,445	301,481	3,096	298,385
1988	553,385	230,080	23,893	206,187	323,305	8,511	314,794
1989	592,917	247,907	27,811	220,096	345,010	6,723	338,287
1990	526,785	174,593	38,497	136,096	352,192	20,700	331,492
1991	522,619	184,745	25,305	159,440	337,874	14,979	322,895
1992	616,810	240,124	39,283	200,841	376,686	20,284	356,402
1993	600,327	223,890	35,109	188,781	376,437	11,206	365,231
1994	511,699	191,960	36,704	155,256	319,739	4,908	314,831
1995	702,157	269,705	45,686	224,019	432,452	13,002	419,450
1996	632,504	246,828	29,566	217,262	385,676	10,339	375,337
1997	601,060	215,188	31,656	183,532	385,872	6,351	379,521
1998	646,011	249,420	52,144	197,276	396,591	6,210	390,381
1999	664,341	242,185	29,664	212,521	422,156	12,690	409,466
2000	666,838	228,153	13,894	214,259	438,685	6,058	432,627
2001	592,337	199,186	14,767	184,419	393,151	2,086	391,065
2002	609,554	228,675	36,053	192,622	380,879	3,178	377,701
2003	687,732	256,828	42,997	213,831	430,904	1,973	428,931
2004	612,905	244,167	33,124	211,043	368,738	1,922	366,816
2005	665,987	320,098	56,934	263,164	345,889	1,450	344,439
2006	664,336	317,261	61,429	255,832	347,075	2,381	344,694

Table A.9b—Trends in pulpwood production by species group, Kentucky, 1962 to 2006

Year	Total production	Roundwood Total	Softwood	Hardwood	Residues Total	Softwood	Hardwood
				green tons			
1953			No data available for 1953 through 1961				
1954							
1955							
1956							
1957							
1958							
1959							
1960							
1961							
1962	225,018	212,693	90,974	121,719	12,325	0	12,325
1963	236,814	221,733	93,185	128,548	15,081	0	15,081
1964	253,814	232,810	96,671	136,139	21,004	1,481	19,523
1965	270,027	245,848	99,120	146,728	24,179	1,698	22,481
1966	420,315	352,732	110,244	242,488	67,583	0	67,583
1967	420,207	240,594	75,346	165,248	179,613	16,650	162,964
1968	461,555	229,522	71,582	157,940	232,033	8,208	223,824
1969	438,873	231,432	74,293	157,139	207,441	16,628	190,813
1970	626,926	320,507	58,388	262,119	306,419	11,356	295,063
1971	806,529	491,190	66,982	424,208	315,339	10,132	305,206
1972	841,162	455,126	66,444	388,682	386,035	12,290	373,746
1973	1,209,798	642,603	91,838	550,766	567,194	22,417	544,777
1974	1,018,701	370,200	66,960	303,240	648,501	21,405	627,096
1975	654,778	178,620	32,454	146,166	476,158	15,936	460,223
1976	666,347	174,697	26,247	148,450	491,650	16,878	474,771
1977	705,923	175,113	21,368	153,745	530,810	18,288	512,523
1978	707,189	141,677	16,500	125,177	565,513	10,871	554,642
1979	867,729	168,681	20,841	147,840	699,048	21,888	677,160
1980	900,619	244,295	35,681	208,614	656,324	15,392	640,932
1981	847,785	215,586	31,901	183,686	632,199	5,534	626,665
1982	935,741	287,605	38,918	248,688	648,135	49,084	599,052
1983	1,327,978	377,818	52,691	325,128	950,160	162,588	787,572
1984	1,340,518	342,187	37,816	304,371	998,331	61,121	937,210
1985	1,263,558	358,108	48,784	309,324	905,450	5,762	899,688
1986	991,832	469,425	69,263	400,162	522,407	6,744	515,663
1987	1,425,825	682,860	93,614	589,246	742,965	7,446	735,519
1988	1,438,271	641,835	64,511	577,324	796,436	20,469	775,967
1989	1,541,405	691,359	75,090	616,269	850,046	16,169	833,877
1990	1,351,922	485,011	103,942	381,069	866,911	49,784	817,128
1991	1,346,716	514,756	68,324	446,432	831,961	36,024	795,936
1992	1,595,733	668,419	106,064	562,355	927,314	48,783	878,531
1993	1,550,626	623,381	94,794	528,587	927,245	26,950	900,294
1994	1,321,680	533,818	99,101	434,717	787,862	11,804	776,058
1995	1,815,819	750,605	123,352	627,253	1,065,214	31,270	1,033,944
1996	1,638,233	688,162	79,828	608,334	950,071	24,865	925,206
1997	1,550,154	599,361	85,471	513,890	950,793	15,274	935,519
1998	1,670,386	693,162	140,789	552,373	977,224	14,935	962,289
1999	1,715,005	675,152	80,093	595,059	1,039,853	30,519	1,009,334
2000	1,718,434	637,439	37,514	599,925	1,080,995	14,569	1,066,426
2001	1,525,236	556,244	39,871	516,373	968,992	5,017	963,975
2002	1,575,361	636,685	97,343	539,342	938,676	7,643	931,033
2003	1,776,879	714,819	116,092	598,727	1,062,060	4,745	1,057,315
2004	1,589,179	680,355	89,435	590,920	908,824	4,622	904,201
2005	1,743,110	890,581	153,722	736,859	852,529	3,487	849,042
2006	1,737,585	882,188	165,858	716,330	855,397	5,726	849,671

Table A.9c—Trends in pulpwood production by species group, Kentucky, 1962 to 2006

Year	Total production	Roundwood			Residues		
		Total	Softwood	Hardwood	Total	Softwood	Hardwood
				thousand cubic feet			
1953				No data available for 1953 through 1961			
1954							
1955							
1956							
1957							
1958							
1959							
1960							
1961							
1962	6,040	5,723	2,594	3,129	317	0	317
1963	6,875	6,441	2,759	3,681	434	0	434
1964	7,368	6,761	2,863	3,899	606	44	562
1965	7,835	7,137	2,935	4,202	698	50	648
1966	12,156	10,209	3,265	6,944	1,947	0	1,947
1967	12,153	6,963	2,231	4,732	5,190	495	4,695
1968	13,335	6,643	2,120	4,523	6,692	244	6,448
1969	12,691	6,700	2,200	4,500	5,991	495	5,497
1970	18,073	9,235	1,729	7,506	8,838	338	8,500
1971	23,225	14,132	1,983	12,148	9,093	301	8,792
1972	24,230	13,098	1,968	11,131	11,132	366	10,767
1973	34,852	18,492	2,720	15,772	16,360	667	15,694
1974	28,352	11,313	2,108	9,205	17,039	630	16,409
1975	19,012	5,138	962	4,176	13,875	472	13,402
1976	19,345	5,019	778	4,241	14,326	500	13,826
1977	20,493	5,026	633	4,393	15,467	542	14,926
1978	20,540	4,065	489	3,576	16,474	322	16,152
1979	25,210	4,842	618	4,224	20,369	649	19,720
1980	26,139	7,018	1,057	5,960	19,121	456	18,665
1981	24,607	6,193	945	5,248	18,413	164	18,250
1982	27,150	8,250	1,153	7,097	18,900	1,454	17,445
1983	38,603	10,851	1,561	9,289	27,753	4,817	22,935
1984	38,921	9,817	1,120	8,696	29,104	1,811	27,293
1985	36,654	10,283	1,445	8,838	26,371	171	26,200
1986	29,545	14,328	2,181	12,148	15,217	200	15,017
1987	41,250	19,610	2,774	16,836	21,640	221	21,420
1988	39,901	17,423	1,745	15,678	22,478	555	21,923
1989	42,764	18,766	2,031	16,736	23,998	439	23,559
1990	37,596	13,160	2,811	10,348	24,436	1,350	23,086
1991	37,436	13,971	1,848	12,123	23,464	977	22,487
1992	44,284	18,140	2,868	15,272	26,144	1,323	24,821
1993	43,085	16,918	2,564	14,355	26,167	731	25,436
1994	36,731	14,485	2,680	11,805	22,246	320	21,926
1995	50,430	20,370	3,336	17,034	30,060	848	29,212
1996	45,493	18,679	2,159	16,520	26,814	674	26,140
1997	43,706	16,861	2,359	14,502	26,845	414	26,431
1998	47,066	19,473	3,885	15,588	27,592	405	27,187
1999	48,828	19,484	2,162	17,322	29,344	828	28,516
2000	49,001	18,476	1,013	17,464	30,525	395	30,129
2001	44,467	17,096	1,074	16,022	27,371	136	27,235
2002	45,868	19,357	2,622	16,735	26,512	207	26,304
2003	51,384	21,383	3,143	18,240	30,001	129	29,872
2004	44,444	18,772	2,421	16,351	25,672	125	25,546
2005	48,138	24,551	4,162	20,389	23,587	94	23,493
2006	47,977	24,311	4,491	19,821	23,665	155	23,510

Table A.10a—Trends in pulpwood production by species group, Louisiana, 1953 to 2006

Year	Total production	Roundwood Total	Softwood	Hardwood	Residues Total	Softwood	Hardwood
				standard cords			
1953	1,381,951	1,375,500	1,178,968	196,532	6,451	2,329	4,122
1954	1,515,871	1,504,207	1,265,232	238,975	11,664	7,928	3,736
1955	1,684,423	1,650,152	1,366,628	283,524	34,271	23,722	10,549
1956	1,648,466	1,574,218	1,289,382	284,836	74,248	68,388	5,860
1957	1,564,184	1,440,223	1,180,811	259,412	123,961	113,809	10,152
1958	1,583,597	1,438,215	1,207,549	230,666	145,382	125,657	19,725
1959	1,799,605	1,612,062	1,297,349	314,713	187,543	160,199	27,344
1960	1,856,941	1,645,599	1,290,963	354,636	211,342	182,394	28,948
1961	1,837,476	1,630,277	1,306,222	324,055	207,199	182,577	24,622
1962	2,006,279	1,782,844	1,375,952	406,892	223,435	204,501	18,934
1963	2,238,224	1,968,521	1,502,990	465,531	269,703	242,601	27,102
1964	2,399,555	2,109,052	1,584,041	525,011	290,503	258,189	32,314
1965	2,453,867	2,096,334	1,540,740	555,594	357,533	323,239	34,294
1966	2,675,175	2,200,465	1,653,781	546,684	474,710	432,797	41,913
1967	2,661,905	2,049,588	1,473,036	576,552	612,317	545,205	67,112
1968	3,011,548	2,274,760	1,659,054	615,706	736,788	623,710	113,078
1969	3,596,288	2,719,531	1,947,957	771,574	876,757	707,880	168,877
1970	3,915,943	2,989,446	2,248,319	741,127	926,497	637,490	289,007
1971	3,995,822	3,164,913	2,348,329	816,584	830,909	687,073	143,836
1972	4,137,652	3,164,764	2,351,233	813,531	972,888	802,903	169,985
1973	4,435,308	3,230,501	2,463,287	767,214	1,204,807	1,006,086	198,721
1974	4,528,205	3,242,265	2,312,474	929,791	1,285,940	1,024,711	261,229
1975	3,567,104	2,755,947	2,108,509	647,438	811,157	634,679	176,478
1976	4,282,898	2,875,665	2,174,420	701,245	1,407,233	1,176,615	230,618
1977	4,340,305	2,730,117	2,027,039	703,078	1,610,188	1,368,311	241,877
1978	4,306,206	3,181,809	2,366,340	815,469	1,124,397	924,003	200,394
1979	4,590,143	3,284,432	2,410,307	874,125	1,305,711	1,031,914	273,797
1980	4,633,408	3,342,685	2,586,542	756,143	1,290,723	830,629	460,094
1981	4,613,637	3,237,431	2,519,680	717,751	1,376,206	774,089	602,117
1982	4,365,827	3,194,185	2,510,721	683,464	1,171,642	717,618	454,024
1983	4,795,215	3,459,317	2,579,835	879,482	1,335,898	1,089,711	246,187
1984	5,085,124	3,733,019	2,643,568	1,089,451	1,352,105	1,008,293	343,812
1985	5,002,954	3,567,126	2,686,079	881,047	1,435,828	1,124,219	311,609
1986	5,430,798	3,731,555	2,773,511	958,044	1,699,243	1,324,822	374,421
1987	5,787,703	4,130,818	3,065,539	1,065,279	1,656,885	1,257,796	399,089
1988	5,899,891	4,224,948	3,205,442	1,019,506	1,674,943	1,247,217	427,726
1989	6,076,294	4,496,187	3,231,615	1,264,572	1,580,107	1,394,693	185,414
1990	6,414,149	4,850,120	3,554,437	1,295,683	1,564,029	1,381,714	182,315
1991	5,947,992	4,318,915	3,187,171	1,131,744	1,629,077	1,412,389	216,688
1992	6,923,629	4,461,523	3,107,909	1,353,614	2,462,106	1,889,883	572,223
1993	7,122,313	4,581,342	3,154,839	1,426,503	2,540,971	1,975,783	565,188
1994	7,311,236	4,916,641	3,237,563	1,679,078	2,394,595	2,101,983	292,612
1995	7,316,055	4,904,548	3,389,883	1,514,665	2,411,507	2,057,712	353,795
1996	6,735,062	4,355,960	3,138,574	1,217,386	2,379,102	2,045,267	333,835
1997	6,965,318	4,371,937	3,078,518	1,293,419	2,593,381	2,175,058	418,323
1998	7,445,761	4,592,870	3,332,871	1,259,999	2,852,891	2,326,471	526,420
1999	6,743,326	4,787,750	3,421,595	1,366,155	1,955,576	1,614,293	341,283
2000	6,911,533	4,204,584	3,061,850	1,142,734	2,706,949	2,039,442	667,507
2001	6,423,587	3,939,846	2,830,697	1,109,149	2,483,741	1,944,514	539,227
2002	6,369,217	3,642,178	2,638,961	1,003,217	2,727,039	2,140,180	586,859
2003	5,766,839	4,153,436	3,130,897	1,022,539	1,613,403	1,448,362	165,041
2004	6,018,530	4,404,886	3,353,734	1,051,152	1,613,644	1,484,153	129,491
2005	6,243,813	4,626,553	3,531,955	1,094,598	1,617,260	1,452,888	164,372
2006	6,340,364	4,661,369	3,501,770	1,159,599	1,678,995	1,478,203	200,792

Table A.10b—Trends in pulpwood production by species group, Louisiana, 1953 to 2006

Year	Total production	Roundwood			Residues		
		Total	Softwood	Hardwood	Total	Softwood	Hardwood
				green tons			
1953	3,749,265	3,733,503	3,183,214	550,290	15,762	5,601	10,161
1954	4,113,532	4,085,256	3,416,126	669,130	28,276	19,067	9,209
1955	4,566,817	4,483,763	3,689,896	793,867	83,055	57,051	26,003
1956	4,457,790	4,278,872	3,481,331	797,541	178,918	164,473	14,445
1957	4,213,279	3,914,543	3,188,190	726,354	298,735	273,711	25,025
1958	4,257,074	3,906,247	3,260,382	645,865	350,827	302,205	48,622
1959	4,836,720	4,384,039	3,502,842	881,196	452,682	385,279	67,403
1960	4,988,595	4,478,581	3,485,600	992,981	510,014	438,658	71,357
1961	4,933,944	4,434,153	3,526,799	907,354	499,791	439,098	60,693
1962	5,392,865	4,854,368	3,715,070	1,139,298	538,497	491,825	46,672
1963	6,011,822	5,361,560	4,058,073	1,303,487	650,262	583,455	66,806
1964	6,447,540	5,746,942	4,276,911	1,470,031	700,599	620,945	79,654
1965	6,577,586	5,715,661	4,159,998	1,555,663	861,925	777,390	84,535
1966	7,140,116	5,995,924	4,465,209	1,530,715	1,144,192	1,040,877	103,316
1967	7,068,192	5,591,543	3,977,197	1,614,346	1,476,649	1,311,218	165,431
1968	7,982,182	6,203,423	4,479,446	1,723,977	1,778,760	1,500,023	278,737
1969	9,538,624	7,419,891	5,259,484	2,160,407	2,118,733	1,702,451	416,282
1970	10,391,183	8,145,617	6,070,461	2,075,156	2,245,566	1,533,163	712,402
1971	10,633,890	8,626,924	6,340,488	2,286,435	2,006,966	1,652,411	354,556
1972	10,976,211	8,626,216	6,348,329	2,277,887	2,349,995	1,930,982	419,013
1973	11,708,558	8,799,074	6,650,875	2,148,199	2,909,484	2,419,637	489,847
1974	11,955,454	8,847,095	6,243,680	2,603,415	3,108,359	2,464,430	643,929
1975	9,467,222	7,505,801	5,692,974	1,812,826	1,961,421	1,526,403	435,018
1976	11,232,652	7,834,420	5,870,934	1,963,486	3,398,232	2,829,759	568,473
1977	11,328,638	7,441,624	5,473,005	1,968,618	3,887,015	3,290,788	596,227
1978	11,388,630	8,672,431	6,389,118	2,283,313	2,716,198	2,222,227	493,971
1979	12,112,042	8,955,379	6,507,829	2,447,550	3,156,663	2,481,753	674,910
1980	12,232,658	9,100,864	6,983,663	2,117,200	3,131,794	1,997,663	1,134,132
1981	12,158,741	8,812,839	6,803,136	2,009,703	3,345,902	1,861,684	1,484,218
1982	11,537,686	8,692,646	6,778,947	1,913,699	2,845,040	1,725,871	1,119,169
1983	12,655,710	9,428,104	6,965,555	2,462,550	3,227,606	2,620,755	606,851
1984	13,460,538	10,188,096	7,137,634	3,050,463	3,272,441	2,424,945	847,497
1985	13,191,208	9,719,345	7,252,413	2,466,932	3,471,863	2,703,747	768,116
1986	14,280,148	10,171,003	7,488,480	2,682,523	4,109,145	3,186,197	922,948
1987	15,268,490	11,259,737	8,276,955	2,982,781	4,008,754	3,024,999	983,754
1988	15,563,212	11,509,310	8,654,693	2,854,617	4,053,901	2,999,557	1,054,345
1989	16,077,444	12,266,162	8,725,361	3,540,802	3,811,282	3,354,237	457,046
1990	16,997,321	13,224,892	9,596,980	3,627,912	3,772,429	3,323,022	449,406
1991	15,705,176	11,774,245	8,605,362	3,168,883	3,930,931	3,396,796	534,136
1992	18,137,172	12,181,474	8,391,354	3,790,119	5,955,698	4,545,169	1,410,530
1993	18,657,220	12,512,274	8,518,065	3,994,208	6,144,947	4,751,758	1,393,188
1994	19,219,396	13,442,839	8,741,420	4,701,418	5,776,558	5,055,269	721,289
1995	19,214,648	13,393,746	9,152,684	4,241,062	5,820,902	4,948,797	872,105
1996	17,624,601	11,882,831	8,474,150	3,408,681	5,741,770	4,918,867	822,903
1997	18,195,752	11,933,572	8,311,999	3,621,573	6,262,181	5,231,014	1,031,166
1998	19,419,537	12,526,749	8,998,752	3,527,997	6,892,788	5,595,163	1,297,625
1999	17,787,178	13,063,541	9,238,307	3,825,234	4,723,637	3,882,375	841,263
2000	18,016,913	11,466,650	8,266,995	3,199,655	6,550,263	4,904,858	1,645,405
2001	16,754,250	10,748,499	7,642,882	3,105,617	6,005,751	4,676,556	1,329,195
2002	16,527,943	9,934,202	7,125,195	2,809,008	6,593,740	5,147,133	1,446,607
2003	15,206,668	11,316,531	8,453,422	2,863,109	3,890,137	3,483,311	406,826
2004	15,886,891	11,998,307	9,055,082	2,943,226	3,888,583	3,569,388	319,195
2005	16,500,526	12,601,153	9,536,279	3,064,874	3,899,373	3,494,196	405,177
2006	16,751,687	12,701,656	9,454,779	3,246,877	4,050,030	3,555,078	494,952

Table A.10c—Trends in pulpwood production by species group, Louisiana, 1953 to 2006

Year	Total production	Roundwood			Residues		
		Total	Softwood	Hardwood	Total	Softwood	Hardwood
				thousand cubic feet			
1953	104,623	104,184	88,894	15,290	439	156	282
1954	114,779	113,990	95,398	18,592	788	532	256
1955	127,417	125,101	103,044	22,058	2,316	1,593	723
1956	124,374	119,379	97,219	22,160	4,994	4,593	401
1957	117,554	109,215	89,033	20,182	8,339	7,644	695
1958	118,785	108,995	91,049	17,946	9,790	8,439	1,351
1959	134,936	122,304	97,820	24,484	12,632	10,759	1,873
1960	139,161	124,929	97,338	27,590	14,233	12,250	1,983
1961	137,649	123,700	98,489	25,211	13,949	12,262	1,686
1962	150,434	135,402	103,747	31,656	15,031	13,735	1,297
1963	167,693	149,543	113,325	36,218	18,150	16,293	1,856
1964	191,204	170,308	128,307	42,001	20,896	18,621	2,276
1965	194,974	169,247	124,800	44,447	25,727	23,312	2,415
1966	211,856	177,691	133,956	43,735	34,165	31,213	2,952
1967	209,486	165,440	119,316	46,124	44,046	39,320	4,726
1968	236,584	183,640	134,383	49,256	52,945	44,982	7,963
1969	282,455	219,510	157,784	61,726	62,945	51,052	11,892
1970	307,731	241,404	182,114	59,290	66,328	45,976	20,352
1971	315,222	255,541	190,214	65,327	59,681	49,552	10,129
1972	325,408	255,532	190,450	65,082	69,876	57,905	11,970
1973	347,456	260,903	199,526	61,377	86,553	72,559	13,994
1974	332,354	245,959	173,436	72,524	86,394	68,456	17,938
1975	263,157	208,638	158,138	50,500	54,518	42,400	12,118
1976	312,219	217,779	163,082	54,697	94,441	78,604	15,836
1977	314,888	206,868	152,028	54,840	108,020	91,411	16,609
1978	316,571	241,082	177,476	63,607	75,489	61,729	13,761
1979	336,693	248,955	180,773	68,182	87,739	68,938	18,801
1980	340,054	252,970	193,991	58,979	87,084	55,491	31,594
1981	338,020	244,961	188,976	55,985	93,060	51,713	41,346
1982	320,732	241,614	188,304	53,310	79,118	47,941	31,177
1983	351,791	262,087	193,488	68,600	89,704	72,799	16,905
1984	366,812	277,645	194,302	83,343	89,167	66,012	23,155
1985	359,415	264,827	197,427	67,400	94,588	73,602	20,986
1986	389,095	277,143	203,853	73,290	111,952	86,735	25,216
1987	416,036	306,811	225,317	81,494	109,225	82,347	26,878
1988	424,053	313,592	235,600	77,992	110,461	81,655	28,806
1989	438,060	334,263	237,524	96,740	103,797	91,310	12,487
1990	463,109	360,371	261,251	99,120	102,739	90,460	12,278
1991	416,555	311,576	226,719	84,857	104,979	90,675	14,303
1992	481,676	322,574	221,081	101,493	159,102	121,330	37,772
1993	495,530	331,377	224,419	106,958	164,152	126,845	37,307
1994	510,462	356,200	230,304	125,896	154,262	134,947	19,315
1995	510,166	354,707	241,139	113,568	155,459	132,105	23,353
1996	467,883	314,541	223,263	91,278	153,342	131,306	22,036
1997	483,221	315,970	218,990	96,979	167,252	139,639	27,613
1998	515,665	331,557	237,084	94,473	184,108	149,359	34,748
1999	475,273	349,108	246,672	102,436	126,165	103,638	22,528
2000	481,414	306,421	220,737	85,684	174,993	130,932	44,061
2001	447,669	287,238	204,073	83,165	160,431	124,838	35,594
2002	442,452	266,315	191,096	75,219	176,137	137,400	38,738
2003	407,265	303,386	226,719	76,668	103,879	92,985	10,894
2004	425,498	321,668	242,855	78,813	103,830	95,283	8,548
2005	440,829	336,558	254,488	82,070	104,270	93,421	10,850
2006	447,559	339,257	252,313	86,944	108,302	95,048	13,254

Table A.11a—Trends in pulpwood production by species group, Mississippi, 1953 to 2006

Year	Total production	Roundwood			Residues		
		Total	Softwood	Hardwood	Total	Softwood	Hardwood
				standard cords			
1953	1,931,993	1,922,975	1,273,396	649,579	9,018	3,256	5,762
1954	1,979,048	1,963,819	1,217,330	746,489	15,229	10,352	4,877
1955	1,948,131	1,908,495	1,028,393	880,102	39,636	27,436	12,200
1956	2,135,735	2,069,033	1,191,236	877,797	66,702	6,529	60,173
1957	2,075,702	1,995,761	1,105,845	889,916	79,941	28,328	51,613
1958	1,885,014	1,786,082	1,035,814	750,268	98,932	49,151	49,781
1959	2,015,775	1,875,544	1,024,294	851,250	140,231	93,570	46,661
1960	1,973,621	1,774,353	956,066	818,287	199,268	152,681	46,587
1961	1,918,772	1,718,896	889,341	829,555	199,876	155,906	43,970
1962	2,100,022	1,831,917	858,643	973,274	268,105	206,177	61,928
1963	1,993,193	1,706,207	683,166	1,023,041	286,986	214,087	72,899
1964	2,157,718	1,801,882	941,909	859,973	355,836	273,823	82,013
1965	2,263,278	1,878,769	1,035,453	843,316	384,509	303,972	80,537
1966	2,949,485	2,475,287	1,560,287	915,000	474,198	353,320	120,878
1967	2,924,515	2,345,968	1,460,377	885,591	578,547	449,680	128,867
1968	3,954,541	3,197,922	2,263,820	934,102	756,619	579,183	177,436
1969	5,071,254	4,128,550	3,023,479	1,105,071	942,704	678,194	264,510
1970	5,053,968	4,124,346	3,073,615	1,050,731	929,622	671,144	258,478
1971	4,679,732	3,599,839	2,624,614	975,225	1,079,893	830,921	248,972
1972	4,584,387	3,545,499	2,367,567	1,177,932	1,038,888	793,786	245,102
1973	5,319,691	3,833,586	2,295,000	1,538,586	1,486,105	1,165,878	320,227
1974	6,032,173	4,502,653	2,782,046	1,720,607	1,529,520	1,150,836	378,684
1975	4,916,238	3,279,001	2,117,375	1,161,626	1,637,237	1,330,428	306,809
1976	5,342,286	3,556,079	2,274,924	1,281,155	1,786,207	1,404,588	381,619
1977	5,211,959	3,411,416	2,276,722	1,134,694	1,800,543	1,429,926	370,617
1978	5,529,953	3,620,209	2,198,205	1,422,004	1,909,744	1,518,327	391,417
1979	7,287,008	4,397,897	2,855,614	1,542,283	2,889,111	2,333,514	555,597
1980	6,013,679	4,129,506	2,606,074	1,523,432	1,884,173	1,504,001	380,172
1981	5,873,316	3,932,699	2,584,268	1,348,431	1,940,617	1,496,092	444,525
1982	5,362,187	3,485,884	2,236,844	1,249,040	1,876,303	1,442,187	434,116
1983	5,634,344	4,081,144	2,313,259	1,767,885	1,553,200	1,268,592	284,608
1984	5,910,002	4,239,583	2,475,609	1,763,974	1,670,419	1,307,914	362,505
1985	5,674,230	3,838,994	2,236,382	1,602,612	1,835,236	1,359,028	476,208
1986	7,129,031	4,935,591	2,979,353	1,956,238	2,193,440	1,522,724	670,716
1987	6,955,184	4,649,703	2,604,435	2,045,268	2,305,481	1,546,488	758,993
1988	7,235,162	4,635,110	2,538,608	2,096,502	2,600,052	1,733,022	867,030
1989	7,498,726	5,273,401	2,805,838	2,467,563	2,225,325	1,664,098	561,227
1990	8,020,290	5,631,572	3,249,299	2,382,273	2,388,718	1,767,096	621,622
1991	8,149,830	5,825,057	3,442,725	2,382,332	2,324,773	1,936,184	388,589
1992	7,581,570	5,359,373	2,851,940	2,507,433	2,222,197	1,927,204	294,993
1993	7,799,634	5,310,053	2,812,016	2,498,037	2,489,581	2,109,989	379,592
1994	7,863,261	5,589,472	2,966,116	2,623,356	2,273,789	1,832,586	441,203
1995	8,363,213	6,035,568	2,842,347	3,193,221	2,327,645	1,713,577	614,068
1996	7,958,954	5,736,522	2,631,606	3,104,916	2,222,432	1,682,873	539,559
1997	9,372,268	6,338,646	2,958,189	3,380,457	3,033,622	2,351,971	681,651
1998	9,040,826	6,164,940	3,374,046	2,790,894	2,875,886	2,263,563	612,323
1999	8,274,401	5,441,577	3,105,649	2,335,928	2,832,824	2,389,639	443,185
2000	7,691,844	4,718,307	2,755,310	1,962,997	2,973,537	2,327,167	646,370
2001	6,888,522	4,252,450	2,695,930	1,556,520	2,636,072	2,212,634	423,438
2002	6,599,840	3,859,734	2,290,210	1,569,524	2,740,106	2,285,770	454,336
2003	6,861,807	4,085,465	2,897,525	1,187,940	2,776,342	2,249,856	526,486
2004	7,333,993	5,234,604	3,366,190	1,868,414	2,099,389	1,978,399	120,990
2005	6,872,449	4,946,577	3,254,837	1,691,740	1,925,872	1,766,305	159,567
2006	7,081,706	5,018,392	3,411,027	1,607,365	2,063,314	1,857,479	205,835

Table A.11b—Trends in pulpwood production by species group, Mississippi, 1953 to 2006

Year	Total production	Roundwood Total	Softwood	Hardwood	Residues Total	Softwood	Hardwood
				green tons			
1953	5,279,024	5,256,990	3,438,169	1,818,821	22,034	7,831	14,203
1954	5,413,879	5,376,960	3,286,791	2,090,169	36,918	24,897	12,022
1955	5,337,003	5,240,947	2,776,661	2,464,286	96,057	65,984	30,073
1956	5,838,197	5,674,169	3,216,337	2,457,832	164,029	15,702	148,326
1957	5,672,901	5,477,546	2,985,782	2,491,765	195,355	68,129	127,226
1958	5,138,367	4,897,448	2,796,698	2,100,750	240,918	118,208	122,710
1959	5,489,149	5,149,094	2,765,594	2,383,500	340,055	225,036	115,019
1960	5,354,617	4,872,582	2,581,378	2,291,204	482,035	367,198	114,837
1961	5,207,315	4,723,975	2,401,221	2,322,754	483,340	374,954	108,386
1962	5,692,012	5,043,503	2,318,336	2,725,167	648,508	495,856	152,653
1963	5,403,638	4,709,063	1,844,548	2,864,515	694,575	514,879	179,696
1964	5,811,785	4,951,079	2,543,154	2,407,924	860,706	658,544	202,162
1965	6,086,584	5,157,008	2,795,723	2,361,285	929,576	731,053	198,524
1966	7,922,474	6,774,775	4,212,775	2,562,000	1,147,699	849,735	297,964
1967	7,821,810	6,422,673	3,943,018	2,479,655	1,399,138	1,081,480	317,657
1968	10,558,114	8,727,800	6,112,314	2,615,486	1,830,315	1,392,935	437,380
1969	13,540,666	11,257,592	8,163,393	3,094,199	2,283,074	1,631,057	652,017
1970	13,492,057	11,240,807	8,298,761	2,942,047	2,251,250	1,614,101	637,148
1971	12,429,169	9,817,088	7,086,458	2,730,630	2,612,081	1,998,365	613,716
1972	12,203,872	9,690,641	6,392,431	3,298,210	2,513,232	1,909,055	604,176
1973	14,097,837	10,504,541	6,196,500	4,308,041	3,593,296	2,803,937	789,360
1974	16,030,440	12,329,224	7,511,524	4,817,700	3,701,217	2,767,761	933,456
1975	12,925,429	8,969,465	5,716,913	3,252,553	3,955,964	3,199,679	756,284
1976	14,048,254	9,729,529	6,142,295	3,587,234	4,318,725	3,378,034	940,691
1977	13,676,836	9,324,293	6,147,149	3,177,143	4,352,543	3,438,972	913,571
1978	14,533,184	9,916,765	5,935,154	3,981,611	4,616,419	3,651,576	964,843
1979	19,010,198	12,028,550	7,710,158	4,318,392	6,981,648	5,612,101	1,369,547
1980	15,856,256	11,302,009	7,036,400	4,265,610	4,554,246	3,617,122	937,124
1981	15,446,986	10,753,130	6,977,524	3,775,607	4,693,855	3,598,101	1,095,754
1982	14,075,346	9,536,791	6,039,479	3,497,312	4,538,556	3,468,460	1,070,096
1983	14,948,400	11,195,877	6,245,799	4,950,078	3,752,522	3,050,964	701,559
1984	15,662,379	11,623,272	6,684,144	4,939,127	4,039,108	3,145,533	893,575
1985	14,967,860	10,525,545	6,038,231	4,487,314	4,442,315	3,268,462	1,173,853
1986	18,837,186	13,521,720	8,044,253	5,477,466	5,315,466	3,662,151	1,653,315
1987	18,348,946	12,758,725	7,031,975	5,726,750	5,590,221	3,719,304	1,870,918
1988	19,029,594	12,724,447	6,854,242	5,870,206	6,305,147	4,167,918	2,137,229
1989	19,870,519	14,484,939	7,575,763	6,909,176	5,385,580	4,002,156	1,383,425
1990	21,225,636	15,443,472	8,773,107	6,670,364	5,782,164	4,249,866	1,532,298
1991	21,580,282	15,965,887	9,295,358	6,670,530	5,614,394	4,656,523	957,872
1992	20,083,134	14,721,050	7,700,238	7,020,812	5,362,083	4,634,926	727,158
1993	20,597,165	14,586,947	7,592,443	6,994,504	6,010,218	5,074,524	935,694
1994	20,848,845	15,353,910	8,008,513	7,345,397	5,494,935	4,407,369	1,087,565
1995	22,250,186	16,615,356	7,674,337	8,941,019	5,634,830	4,121,153	1,513,678
1996	21,176,424	15,799,101	7,105,336	8,693,765	5,377,323	4,047,310	1,330,013
1997	24,789,150	17,452,390	7,987,110	9,465,280	7,336,760	5,656,490	1,680,270
1998	23,877,673	16,924,427	9,109,924	7,814,503	6,953,245	5,443,869	1,509,376
1999	21,765,384	14,925,851	8,385,252	6,540,598	6,839,533	5,747,082	1,092,451
2000	20,125,867	12,935,729	7,439,337	5,496,392	7,190,139	5,596,837	1,593,302
2001	18,002,426	11,637,267	7,279,011	4,358,256	6,365,159	5,321,385	1,043,775
2002	17,195,449	10,578,234	6,183,567	4,394,667	6,617,215	5,497,277	1,119,938
2003	17,858,241	11,149,550	7,823,318	3,326,232	6,708,692	5,410,904	1,297,788
2004	19,376,562	14,320,272	9,088,713	5,231,559	5,056,290	4,758,050	298,240
2005	18,166,228	13,524,932	8,788,060	4,736,872	4,641,296	4,247,964	393,333
2006	18,685,015	13,710,395	9,209,773	4,500,622	4,974,620	4,467,237	507,383

Table A.11c—Trends in pulpwood production by species group, Mississippi, 1953 to 2006

Year	Total production	Roundwood			Residues		
		Total	Softwood	Hardwood	Total	Softwood	Hardwood
		thousand cubic feet					
1953	146,785	146,172	95,505	50,667	613	218	396
1954	150,552	149,526	91,300	58,226	1,026	692	335
1955	148,448	145,777	77,129	68,648	2,671	1,833	838
1956	162,379	157,811	89,343	68,468	4,568	436	4,132
1957	166,446	160,767	89,573	71,193	5,679	2,044	3,635
1958	150,975	143,922	83,901	60,021	7,052	3,546	3,506
1959	161,105	151,068	82,968	68,100	10,037	6,751	3,286
1960	157,201	142,904	77,441	65,463	14,297	11,016	3,281
1961	152,746	138,401	72,037	66,364	14,345	11,249	3,097
1962	166,649	147,412	69,550	77,862	19,237	14,876	4,362
1963	157,760	137,180	55,336	81,843	20,581	15,446	5,134
1964	170,625	145,092	76,295	68,798	25,532	19,756	5,776
1965	178,941	151,337	83,872	67,465	27,604	21,932	5,672
1966	233,589	199,583	126,383	73,200	34,005	25,492	8,513
1967	230,658	189,138	118,291	70,847	41,520	32,444	9,076
1968	312,382	258,098	183,369	74,728	54,285	41,788	12,497
1969	400,868	333,307	244,902	88,406	67,561	48,932	18,629
1970	399,649	333,021	248,963	84,058	66,627	48,423	18,204
1971	368,097	290,612	212,594	78,018	77,486	59,951	17,535
1972	360,541	286,007	191,773	94,234	74,534	57,272	17,262
1973	415,653	308,982	185,895	123,087	106,671	84,118	22,553
1974	472,697	362,994	225,346	137,649	109,703	83,033	26,670
1975	382,036	264,437	171,507	92,930	117,599	95,990	21,608
1976	414,979	286,761	184,269	102,492	128,218	101,341	26,877
1977	393,810	268,360	177,584	90,776	125,450	99,348	26,102
1978	418,277	285,220	171,460	113,760	133,057	105,490	27,567
1979	547,378	346,121	222,738	123,383	201,257	162,127	39,130
1980	456,418	325,148	203,274	121,875	131,270	104,495	26,775
1981	444,700	309,447	201,573	107,874	135,252	103,945	31,307
1982	405,171	274,397	174,474	99,923	130,774	100,200	30,574
1983	430,049	321,865	180,434	141,431	108,184	88,139	20,045
1984	450,617	334,215	193,098	141,118	116,402	90,871	25,531
1985	430,608	302,647	174,438	128,209	127,961	94,422	33,539
1986	541,922	388,889	232,390	156,499	153,033	105,796	47,238
1987	507,583	352,818	195,333	157,486	154,764	103,314	51,450
1988	526,376	351,826	190,396	161,431	174,549	115,776	58,774
1989	549,655	400,440	210,438	190,002	149,215	111,171	38,044
1990	587,323	427,132	243,697	183,435	160,190	118,052	42,138
1991	597,333	441,644	258,204	183,440	155,689	129,348	26,341
1992	555,713	406,968	213,896	193,072	148,745	128,748	19,997
1993	569,941	403,250	210,901	192,349	166,691	140,959	25,732
1994	576,792	424,457	222,459	201,998	152,335	122,427	29,908
1995	606,737	453,715	208,192	245,523	153,022	111,822	41,200
1996	577,509	431,490	192,756	238,734	146,019	109,819	36,201
1997	675,813	476,597	216,677	259,920	199,216	153,482	45,734
1998	650,521	461,726	247,137	214,589	188,795	147,713	41,082
1999	589,551	403,876	227,311	176,565	185,674	155,940	29,735
2000	545,276	350,046	201,669	148,377	195,230	151,863	43,367
2001	487,774	314,975	197,323	117,652	172,799	144,389	28,410
2002	466,547	286,903	168,144	118,759	179,644	149,162	30,483
2003	484,760	302,618	212,732	89,886	182,142	146,818	35,323
2004	525,737	388,515	247,141	141,374	137,221	129,104	8,118
2005	491,896	365,927	238,166	127,761	125,969	115,263	10,706
2006	506,006	370,983	249,595	121,388	135,023	121,213	13,810

Table A.12a—Trends in pulpwood production by species group, North Carolina, 1953 to 2006

Year	Total production	Roundwood			Residues		
		Total	Softwood	Hardwood	Total	Softwood	Hardwood
				standard cords			
1953	1,536,121	1,528,929	1,263,147	265,782	7,192	2,597	4,595
1954	1,519,095	1,507,406	1,228,924	278,482	11,689	7,945	3,744
1955	1,606,661	1,573,972	1,273,399	300,573	32,689	22,627	10,062
1956	1,922,344	1,842,162	1,512,071	330,091	80,182	68,833	11,349
1957	1,865,854	1,763,116	1,437,096	326,020	102,738	85,319	17,419
1958	1,896,101	1,705,994	1,342,722	363,272	190,107	174,494	15,613
1959	2,145,846	1,834,074	1,429,454	404,620	311,772	275,526	36,246
1960	2,273,564	1,887,816	1,486,193	401,623	385,748	324,995	60,753
1961	2,291,891	1,879,925	1,430,405	449,520	411,966	342,013	69,953
1962	2,323,956	1,849,909	1,390,173	459,736	474,047	383,325	90,722
1963	2,422,885	1,898,167	1,439,112	459,055	524,718	417,513	107,205
1964	2,624,459	2,070,181	1,527,749	542,432	554,278	436,892	117,386
1965	2,855,686	2,267,889	1,705,240	562,649	587,797	463,220	124,577
1966	3,052,541	2,396,803	1,733,504	663,299	655,738	500,821	154,917
1967	3,156,748	2,445,960	1,719,609	726,351	710,788	527,864	182,924
1968	3,156,124	2,490,249	1,730,798	759,451	665,875	528,011	137,864
1969	3,517,003	2,829,959	1,910,130	919,829	687,044	531,312	155,732
1970	4,107,533	3,415,006	2,381,503	1,033,503	692,527	493,011	199,516
1971	3,654,393	2,827,471	1,854,121	973,350	826,922	608,230	218,692
1972	4,106,205	3,031,629	1,892,951	1,138,678	1,074,576	861,313	213,263
1973	4,232,687	3,082,046	1,874,058	1,207,988	1,150,641	924,121	226,520
1974	4,515,743	3,064,745	1,993,540	1,071,205	1,450,998	1,109,111	341,887
1975	3,700,544	2,427,038	1,571,415	855,623	1,273,506	1,008,990	264,516
1976	4,158,664	2,483,800	1,490,282	993,518	1,674,864	1,394,279	280,585
1977	4,576,159	2,757,816	1,680,674	1,077,142	1,818,343	1,491,823	326,520
1978	4,639,185	2,925,718	1,674,390	1,251,328	1,713,467	1,374,588	338,879
1979	4,478,454	2,701,143	1,604,781	1,096,362	1,777,311	1,298,714	478,597
1980	4,849,799	3,146,698	1,962,540	1,184,158	1,703,101	1,255,918	447,183
1981	4,900,406	3,213,614	1,956,496	1,257,118	1,686,792	1,197,676	489,116
1982	4,570,164	3,077,240	1,834,991	1,242,249	1,492,924	1,070,709	422,215
1983	4,780,889	3,004,895	1,750,470	1,254,425	1,775,994	1,114,507	661,487
1984	5,234,716	3,394,340	2,005,061	1,389,279	1,840,376	1,338,391	501,985
1985	4,966,691	3,294,854	1,915,292	1,379,562	1,671,837	1,115,314	556,523
1986	5,369,469	3,655,147	2,105,633	1,549,514	1,714,322	1,205,008	509,314
1987	5,766,618	3,889,919	2,290,864	1,599,055	1,876,699	1,356,891	519,808
1988	5,541,067	3,859,327	2,258,567	1,600,760	1,681,740	1,130,211	551,529
1989	5,147,527	3,565,429	2,108,912	1,456,517	1,582,098	1,044,284	537,814
1990	5,637,129	4,165,324	2,525,592	1,639,732	1,471,805	964,692	507,113
1991	6,602,427	4,828,413	3,016,347	1,812,066	1,774,014	1,145,493	628,521
1992	6,351,360	4,525,533	2,802,342	1,723,191	1,825,827	1,291,816	534,011
1993	6,658,851	4,799,848	2,767,513	2,032,335	1,859,003	1,293,706	565,297
1994	6,480,047	4,609,117	2,553,696	2,055,421	1,870,930	1,331,409	539,521
1995	6,357,309	4,314,811	2,552,924	1,761,887	2,042,498	1,444,922	597,576
1996	5,578,818	3,759,705	2,291,755	1,467,950	1,819,113	1,258,232	560,881
1997	7,215,893	4,642,407	2,659,995	1,982,412	2,573,486	1,480,944	1,092,542
1998	6,868,987	4,466,827	2,597,347	1,869,480	2,402,160	1,509,554	892,606
1999	5,855,652	3,568,704	2,213,856	1,354,848	2,286,948	1,445,378	841,570
2000	5,592,654	3,309,538	2,018,184	1,291,354	2,283,116	1,427,318	855,798
2001	5,480,809	3,170,504	1,897,562	1,272,942	2,310,305	1,418,908	891,397
2002	5,315,913	3,097,702	1,873,267	1,224,435	2,218,211	1,395,197	823,014
2003	4,903,187	3,435,697	2,044,825	1,390,872	1,467,490	1,055,430	412,060
2004	4,803,517	3,637,581	2,033,742	1,603,839	1,165,936	771,326	394,610
2005	5,331,002	3,574,973	1,796,398	1,778,575	1,756,029	1,254,111	501,918
2006	5,176,140	3,389,431	1,885,376	1,504,055	1,786,709	1,195,063	591,646

Table A.12b—Trends in pulpwood production by species group, North Carolina, 1953 to 2006

Year	Total production	Roundwood Total	Softwood	Hardwood	Residues Total	Softwood	Hardwood
				green tons			
1953	4,172,259	4,154,687	3,410,497	744,190	17,572	6,246	11,327
1954	4,126,181	4,097,844	3,318,095	779,750	28,337	19,108	9,229
1955	4,359,002	4,279,782	3,438,177	841,604	79,221	54,418	24,803
1956	5,200,365	5,006,847	4,082,592	924,255	193,519	165,543	27,975
1957	5,041,145	4,793,015	3,880,159	912,856	248,130	205,192	42,938
1958	5,100,655	4,642,511	3,625,349	1,017,162	458,144	419,658	38,486
1959	5,744,448	4,992,462	3,859,526	1,132,936	751,986	662,640	89,346
1960	6,068,635	5,137,266	4,012,721	1,124,544	931,369	781,613	149,756
1961	6,115,725	5,120,750	3,862,094	1,258,656	994,975	822,541	172,434
1962	6,186,254	5,040,728	3,753,467	1,287,261	1,145,526	921,897	223,630
1963	6,439,335	5,170,956	3,885,602	1,285,354	1,268,379	1,004,119	264,260
1964	6,983,814	5,643,732	4,124,922	1,518,810	1,340,082	1,050,725	289,356
1965	7,600,692	6,179,565	4,604,148	1,575,417	1,421,126	1,114,044	307,082
1966	8,124,043	6,537,698	4,680,461	1,857,237	1,586,345	1,204,475	381,870
1967	8,397,148	6,676,727	4,642,944	2,033,783	1,720,421	1,269,513	450,908
1968	8,409,319	6,799,617	4,673,155	2,126,463	1,609,701	1,269,866	339,835
1969	9,394,557	7,732,872	5,157,351	2,575,521	1,661,685	1,277,805	383,879
1970	11,001,365	9,323,867	6,430,058	2,893,808	1,677,498	1,185,691	491,807
1971	9,733,376	7,731,507	5,006,127	2,725,380	2,001,869	1,462,793	539,076
1972	10,896,417	8,299,266	5,110,968	3,188,298	2,597,151	2,071,458	525,693
1973	11,223,206	8,442,323	5,059,957	3,382,366	2,780,883	2,222,511	558,372
1974	11,892,095	8,381,932	5,382,558	2,999,374	3,510,163	2,667,412	842,751
1975	9,717,218	6,638,565	4,242,821	2,395,744	3,078,653	2,426,621	652,032
1976	10,850,495	6,805,612	4,023,761	2,781,850	4,044,883	3,353,241	691,642
1977	11,946,524	7,553,817	4,537,820	3,015,998	4,392,706	3,587,834	804,872
1978	12,165,792	8,024,571	4,520,853	3,503,718	4,141,221	3,305,884	835,337
1979	11,705,871	7,402,722	4,332,909	3,069,814	4,303,149	3,123,407	1,179,742
1980	12,737,289	8,614,500	5,298,858	3,315,642	4,122,789	3,020,483	1,102,306
1981	12,888,551	8,802,470	5,282,539	3,519,930	4,086,082	2,880,411	1,205,671
1982	12,048,588	8,432,773	4,954,476	3,478,297	3,615,815	2,575,055	1,040,760
1983	12,549,614	8,238,659	4,726,269	3,512,390	4,310,955	2,680,389	1,630,565
1984	13,759,869	9,303,646	5,413,665	3,889,981	4,456,223	3,218,830	1,237,393
1985	13,088,221	9,034,062	5,171,288	3,862,774	4,054,159	2,682,330	1,371,829
1986	14,177,352	10,023,848	5,685,209	4,338,639	4,153,503	2,898,044	1,255,459
1987	15,207,336	10,662,687	6,185,333	4,477,354	4,544,650	3,263,323	1,281,327
1988	14,657,935	10,580,259	6,098,131	4,482,128	4,077,676	2,718,157	1,359,519
1989	13,609,525	9,772,310	5,694,062	4,078,248	3,837,215	2,511,503	1,325,712
1990	14,980,466	11,410,348	6,819,098	4,591,250	3,570,118	2,320,084	1,250,034
1991	17,522,137	13,217,922	8,144,137	5,073,785	4,304,215	2,754,911	1,549,304
1992	16,814,413	12,391,258	7,566,323	4,824,935	4,423,155	3,106,817	1,316,337
1993	17,667,643	13,162,823	7,472,285	5,690,538	4,504,820	3,111,363	1,393,457
1994	17,182,116	12,650,158	6,894,979	5,755,179	4,531,958	3,202,039	1,329,919
1995	16,774,241	11,826,178	6,892,895	4,933,284	4,948,062	3,475,037	1,473,025
1996	14,706,618	10,297,999	6,187,739	4,110,260	4,408,620	3,026,048	1,382,572
1997	18,987,526	12,732,740	7,181,987	5,550,754	6,254,786	3,561,670	2,693,116
1998	18,078,132	12,247,381	7,012,837	5,234,544	5,830,751	3,630,477	2,200,274
1999	15,321,590	9,770,986	5,977,411	3,793,574	5,550,604	3,476,134	2,074,470
2000	14,607,130	9,064,888	5,449,097	3,615,791	5,542,242	3,432,700	2,109,542
2001	14,297,422	8,687,655	5,123,417	3,564,238	5,609,767	3,412,474	2,197,294
2002	13,870,417	8,486,239	5,057,821	3,428,418	5,384,178	3,355,449	2,028,730
2003	12,969,506	9,415,469	5,521,028	3,894,442	3,554,037	2,538,309	1,015,728
2004	12,809,605	9,981,853	5,491,103	4,490,749	2,827,753	1,855,039	972,714
2005	14,083,649	9,830,285	4,850,275	4,980,010	4,253,365	3,016,137	1,237,228
2006	13,634,403	9,301,869	5,090,515	4,211,354	4,332,534	2,874,127	1,458,407

Table A.12c—Trends in pulpwood production by species group, North Carolina, 1953 to 2006

Year	Total production	Roundwood			Residues		
		Total	Softwood	Hardwood	Total	Softwood	Hardwood
		thousand cubic feet					
1953	107,962	107,495	87,292	20,203	467	160	307
1954	106,835	106,095	84,927	21,169	740	489	251
1955	112,914	110,848	88,000	22,848	2,066	1,393	673
1956	142,911	137,590	112,499	25,092	5,321	4,562	759
1957	138,523	131,703	106,920	24,782	6,820	5,654	1,166
1958	140,122	127,513	99,899	27,614	12,609	11,564	1,045
1959	157,794	137,109	106,352	30,757	20,685	18,259	2,426
1960	166,706	141,102	110,573	30,529	25,603	21,538	4,066
1961	167,940	140,593	106,423	34,170	27,347	22,666	4,681
1962	169,851	138,376	103,429	34,947	31,475	25,403	6,071
1963	176,809	141,965	107,070	34,895	34,843	27,669	7,174
1964	190,786	154,076	113,665	40,411	36,709	29,057	7,652
1965	207,717	168,788	126,870	41,917	38,929	30,808	8,121
1966	221,797	178,389	128,973	49,416	43,408	33,309	10,099
1967	229,085	182,053	127,939	54,113	47,032	35,107	11,925
1968	229,456	185,351	128,772	56,579	44,105	35,117	8,987
1969	230,839	185,350	128,771	56,579	45,489	35,337	10,152
1970	307,323	261,527	182,608	78,919	45,796	32,789	13,006
1971	271,204	216,495	142,169	74,326	54,709	40,453	14,256
1972	303,284	232,097	145,147	86,950	71,187	57,285	13,903
1973	312,170	235,941	143,698	92,243	76,229	61,462	14,767
1974	341,804	234,658	152,860	81,798	107,146	83,143	24,003
1975	280,037	185,828	120,492	65,336	94,209	75,638	18,571
1976	351,382	227,163	148,968	78,195	124,219	104,520	19,699
1977	360,525	225,768	140,992	84,777	134,757	111,832	22,924
1978	365,786	238,950	140,465	98,486	126,836	103,044	23,792
1979	355,077	224,119	134,625	89,494	130,958	97,356	33,601
1980	386,842	261,298	164,637	96,661	125,544	94,148	31,396
1981	390,868	266,747	164,130	102,616	124,122	89,782	34,340
1982	365,247	255,340	153,937	101,402	109,907	80,264	29,643
1983	384,363	254,374	153,318	101,056	129,989	83,547	46,442
1984	407,858	275,162	163,242	111,920	132,697	97,483	35,214
1985	387,345	267,070	155,933	111,137	120,274	81,235	39,039
1986	422,173	298,677	171,430	127,247	123,496	87,768	35,728
1987	455,830	320,536	194,421	126,115	135,294	98,830	36,464
1988	429,378	308,369	182,120	126,250	121,009	82,320	38,689
1989	398,714	284,925	170,052	114,873	113,788	76,061	37,727
1990	431,522	330,735	203,651	127,084	100,787	65,959	34,827
1991	505,150	383,664	243,223	140,440	121,487	78,321	43,165
1992	473,827	348,827	215,327	133,500	125,001	88,326	36,675
1993	497,379	370,101	212,651	157,450	127,278	88,455	38,823
1994	486,839	358,753	198,479	160,274	128,086	91,033	37,053
1995	471,705	331,871	193,572	138,299	139,834	98,794	41,040
1996	413,545	288,996	173,769	115,226	124,550	86,030	38,520
1997	530,859	354,568	200,833	153,735	176,290	101,257	75,033
1998	505,596	341,080	196,103	144,977	164,515	103,213	61,302
1999	428,467	271,845	164,991	106,854	156,622	98,826	57,797
2000	408,619	252,255	150,408	101,846	156,365	97,591	58,774
2001	401,235	243,001	141,903	101,098	158,235	97,016	61,219
2002	388,694	237,332	140,086	97,245	151,363	95,023	56,339
2003	367,003	266,913	158,359	108,554	100,090	71,883	28,208
2004	362,222	282,676	157,501	125,175	79,546	52,533	27,013
2005	393,435	273,662	136,936	136,726	119,773	85,414	34,359
2006	381,235	259,341	143,719	115,623	121,894	81,393	40,501

Table A.13a—Trends in pulpwood production by species group, Oklahoma, 1953 to 2006

Year	Total production	Roundwood			Residues		
		Total	Softwood	Hardwood	Total	Softwood	Hardwood
				standard cords			
1953	41,220	41,028	41,028	0	192	70	122
1954	33,278	33,022	33,022	0	256	174	82
1955	38,863	38,073	33,673	4,400	790	547	243
1956	74,535	74,535	68,535	6,000	0	0	0
1957	59,904	59,425	51,372	8,053	479	479	0
1958	63,060	46,934	37,999	8,935	16,126	16,126	0
1959	54,838	38,097	29,069	9,028	16,741	16,741	0
1960	53,055	38,593	30,097	8,496	14,462	14,462	0
1961	40,421	22,492	13,317	9,175	17,929	17,929	0
1962	59,230	31,662	10,686	20,976	27,568	27,568	0
1963	64,542	25,140	6,489	18,651	39,402	39,402	0
1964	70,656	23,648	3,904	19,744	47,008	47,008	0
1965	91,679	38,496	8,019	30,477	53,183	53,183	0
1966	117,031	62,245	15,927	46,318	54,786	54,786	0
1967	118,828	59,217	19,513	39,704	59,611	59,068	543
1968	155,360	89,850	40,010	49,840	65,510	63,425	2,085
1969	190,690	117,008	54,975	62,033	73,682	70,414	3,268
1970	196,669	93,078	49,430	43,648	103,591	98,873	4,718
1971	226,311	91,545	54,178	37,367	134,766	130,989	3,777
1972	469,518	285,654	190,791	94,863	183,864	182,586	1,278
1973	616,705	322,097	155,927	166,170	294,608	240,924	53,684
1974	707,087	261,201	119,557	141,644	445,886	386,373	59,513
1975	390,058	158,901	110,453	48,448	231,157	215,782	15,375
1976	521,744	264,411	185,673	78,738	257,333	218,922	38,411
1977	692,105	329,631	231,561	98,070	362,474	362,474	0
1978	613,633	348,752	243,374	105,378	264,881	244,979	19,902
1979	542,506	515,195	406,716	108,479	27,311	23,513	3,798
1980	558,748	386,380	286,503	99,877	172,368	142,286	30,082
1981	425,579	266,874	153,524	113,350	158,705	121,187	37,518
1982	636,042	277,723	203,718	74,005	358,319	290,996	67,323
1983	754,955	127,767	74,409	53,358	627,188	399,677	227,511
1984	608,193	125,380	73,567	51,813	482,813	307,821	174,992
1985	641,778	238,579	72,029	166,550	403,199	382,622	20,577
1986	586,303	104,262	55,501	48,761	482,041	373,314	108,727
1987	608,044	98,822	54,783	44,039	509,222	384,999	124,223
1988	731,208	332,464	131,186	201,278	398,744	390,723	8,021
1989	566,211	220,005	112,499	107,506	346,206	340,485	5,721
1990	1,156,922	838,996	626,710	212,286	317,926	193,683	124,243
1991	1,262,484	1,074,417	856,271	218,146	188,067	149,375	38,692
1992	991,481	847,974	710,312	137,662	143,507	128,511	14,996
1993	541,087	261,852	218,901	42,951	279,235	192,112	87,123
1994	487,880	313,417	240,306	73,111	174,463	154,294	20,169
1995	992,584	572,598	347,933	224,665	419,986	359,424	60,562
1996	775,512	543,890	393,425	150,465	231,622	228,087	3,535
1997	900,797	590,818	445,358	145,460	309,979	289,469	20,510
1998	1,110,860	754,637	527,864	226,773	356,223	326,543	29,680
1999	746,333	665,312	445,002	220,310	81,021	74,755	6,266
2000	751,853	464,131	274,112	190,019	287,722	271,399	16,323
2001	781,956	407,294	226,928	180,366	374,662	366,369	8,293
2002	940,113	608,175	343,073	265,102	331,938	313,857	18,081
2003	818,935	535,130	324,152	210,978	283,805	267,277	16,528
2004	711,656	443,977	267,869	176,108	267,679	251,530	16,149
2005	706,776	441,676	231,767	209,909	265,100	251,873	13,227
2006	652,293	440,117	261,857	178,260	212,176	202,158	10,018

Table A.13b—Trends in pulpwood production by species group, Oklahoma, 1953 to 2006

Year	Total production	Roundwood Total	Roundwood Softwood	Roundwood Hardwood	Residues Total	Residues Softwood	Residues Hardwood
				green tons			
1953	111,245	110,776	110,776	0	469	168	301
1954	89,780	89,159	89,159	0	621	418	202
1955	105,152	103,237	90,917	12,320	1,915	1,316	599
1956	201,845	201,845	185,045	16,800	0	0	0
1957	162,405	161,253	138,704	22,548	1,152	1,152	0
1958	166,398	127,615	102,597	25,018	38,783	38,783	0
1959	144,027	103,765	78,486	25,278	40,262	40,262	0
1960	139,832	105,051	81,262	23,789	34,781	34,781	0
1961	104,765	61,646	35,956	25,690	43,119	43,119	0
1962	153,886	87,585	28,852	58,733	66,301	66,301	0
1963	164,505	69,743	17,520	52,223	94,762	94,762	0
1964	178,878	65,824	10,541	55,283	113,054	113,054	0
1965	234,892	106,987	21,651	85,336	127,905	127,905	0
1966	304,454	172,693	43,003	129,690	131,760	131,760	0
1967	307,253	163,856	52,685	111,171	143,397	142,059	1,338
1968	405,256	247,579	108,027	139,552	157,677	152,537	5,140
1969	499,526	322,125	148,433	173,692	177,401	169,346	8,056
1970	505,095	255,675	133,461	122,214	249,419	237,790	11,630
1971	575,247	250,908	146,281	104,628	324,339	315,029	9,310
1972	1,223,022	780,752	515,136	265,616	442,270	439,119	3,150
1973	1,598,032	886,279	421,003	465,276	711,753	579,422	132,331
1974	1,795,334	719,407	322,804	396,603	1,075,927	929,227	146,700
1975	990,733	433,878	298,223	135,654	556,855	518,956	37,899
1976	1,342,974	721,784	501,317	220,466	621,191	526,507	94,683
1977	1,771,561	899,811	625,215	274,596	871,750	871,750	0
1978	1,590,401	952,168	657,110	295,058	638,233	589,174	49,058
1979	1,467,785	1,401,874	1,098,133	303,741	65,911	56,549	9,362
1980	1,469,564	1,053,214	773,558	279,656	416,350	342,198	74,152
1981	1,115,831	731,895	414,515	317,380	383,937	291,455	92,482
1982	1,623,049	757,253	550,039	207,214	865,797	699,845	165,951
1983	1,872,345	350,307	200,904	149,402	1,522,038	961,223	560,815
1984	1,515,372	343,707	198,631	145,076	1,171,665	740,310	431,355
1985	1,631,747	660,818	194,478	466,340	970,928	920,206	50,722
1986	1,452,216	286,384	149,853	136,531	1,165,832	897,820	268,012
1987	1,503,356	271,223	147,914	123,309	1,232,132	925,923	306,210
1988	1,877,241	917,781	354,202	563,578	959,461	939,689	19,772
1989	1,437,733	604,764	303,747	301,017	832,969	818,866	14,102
1990	3,058,584	2,286,518	1,692,117	594,401	772,067	465,808	306,259
1991	3,377,363	2,922,741	2,311,932	610,809	454,623	359,247	95,376
1992	2,649,330	2,303,296	1,917,842	385,454	346,034	309,069	36,965
1993	1,388,083	711,296	591,033	120,263	676,788	462,029	214,758
1994	1,274,331	853,537	648,826	204,711	420,794	371,077	49,717
1995	2,582,181	1,568,481	939,419	629,062	1,013,700	864,415	149,285
1996	2,040,813	1,483,550	1,062,248	421,302	557,263	548,549	8,714
1997	2,356,485	1,609,755	1,202,467	407,288	746,730	696,173	50,557
1998	2,918,694	2,060,197	1,425,233	634,964	858,497	785,336	73,161
1999	2,013,605	1,818,373	1,201,505	616,868	195,231	179,786	15,446
2000	1,965,106	1,272,156	740,102	532,053	692,951	652,715	40,236
2001	2,019,290	1,117,730	612,706	505,025	901,560	881,117	20,442
2002	2,467,978	1,668,583	926,297	742,286	799,396	754,826	44,570
2003	2,149,492	1,465,949	875,210	590,738	683,543	642,801	40,742
2004	1,861,086	1,216,349	723,246	493,102	644,737	604,930	39,807
2005	1,851,875	1,213,516	625,771	587,745	638,359	605,755	32,605
2006	1,717,026	1,206,142	707,014	499,128	510,884	486,190	24,694

Table A.13c—Trends in pulpwood production by species group, Oklahoma, 1953 to 2006

Year	Total production	Roundwood Total	Roundwood Softwood	Roundwood Hardwood	Residues Total	Residues Softwood	Residues Hardwood
				thousand cubic feet			
1953	3,108	3,095	3,095	0	13	5	8
1954	2,508	2,491	2,491	0	17	12	5
1955	2,933	2,880	2,540	340	53	37	16
1956	5,638	5,638	5,171	467	0	0	0
1957	4,535	4,502	3,876	627	32	32	0
1958	4,646	3,562	2,867	695	1,084	1,084	0
1959	4,021	2,896	2,193	702	1,125	1,125	0
1960	3,904	2,932	2,271	661	972	972	0
1961	2,924	1,719	1,005	714	1,205	1,205	0
1962	4,291	2,438	806	1,632	1,853	1,853	0
1963	4,589	1,941	490	1,451	2,648	2,648	0
1964	4,990	1,831	295	1,536	3,159	3,159	0
1965	6,550	2,976	605	2,371	3,574	3,574	0
1966	8,948	4,996	1,290	3,705	3,953	3,953	0
1967	9,057	4,757	1,581	3,176	4,300	4,262	38
1968	11,951	7,228	3,241	3,987	4,723	4,576	147
1969	14,726	9,416	4,453	4,963	5,311	5,080	230
1970	14,962	7,496	4,004	3,492	7,466	7,134	332
1971	17,095	7,378	4,388	2,989	9,717	9,451	266
1972	36,307	23,043	15,454	7,589	13,264	13,174	90
1973	47,087	25,924	12,630	13,294	21,164	17,383	3,781
1974	53,084	21,016	9,684	11,331	32,068	27,877	4,191
1975	29,474	12,822	8,947	3,876	16,652	15,569	1,083
1976	39,839	21,339	15,040	6,299	18,500	15,795	2,705
1977	52,755	26,602	18,756	7,846	26,152	26,152	0
1978	47,220	28,144	19,713	8,430	19,077	17,675	1,402
1979	43,586	41,622	32,944	8,678	1,964	1,696	267
1980	43,581	31,197	23,207	7,990	12,385	10,266	2,119
1981	32,889	21,503	12,435	9,068	11,386	8,744	2,642
1982	48,158	22,422	16,501	5,920	25,737	20,995	4,741
1983	55,156	10,296	6,027	4,269	44,860	28,837	16,023
1984	44,638	10,104	5,959	4,145	34,534	22,209	12,324
1985	48,214	19,158	5,834	13,324	29,055	27,606	1,449
1986	40,371	7,966	4,163	3,803	32,406	24,939	7,466
1987	41,794	7,544	4,109	3,435	34,250	25,720	8,530
1988	52,192	25,539	9,839	15,700	26,653	26,102	551
1989	39,962	16,823	8,437	8,385	23,139	22,746	393
1990	85,032	63,562	47,003	16,558	21,471	12,939	8,532
1991	93,872	81,236	64,220	17,015	12,636	9,979	2,657
1992	73,626	64,011	53,273	10,738	9,615	8,585	1,030
1993	38,553	19,357	16,018	3,340	19,196	12,998	6,198
1994	35,142	23,268	17,584	5,685	11,874	10,439	1,435
1995	71,554	42,927	25,459	17,468	28,626	24,318	4,309
1996	56,170	40,487	28,788	11,699	15,683	15,432	251
1997	64,942	43,898	32,588	11,310	21,044	19,585	1,459
1998	80,462	56,257	38,625	17,632	24,204	22,093	2,112
1999	59,237	53,734	32,508	21,226	5,503	5,058	446
2000	54,752	35,228	20,024	15,204	19,523	18,362	1,161
2001	56,387	31,009	16,577	14,432	25,377	24,787	590
2002	71,439	48,918	27,706	21,212	22,521	21,235	1,286
2003	62,318	43,059	26,178	16,881	19,259	18,083	1,176
2004	53,890	35,724	21,633	14,091	18,167	17,018	1,149
2005	54,591	36,609	19,626	16,983	17,982	17,041	941
2006	50,987	36,596	22,174	14,422	14,390	13,677	713

Table A.14a—Trends in pulpwood production by species group, South Carolina, 1953 to 2006

Year	Total production	Roundwood			Residues		
		Total	Softwood	Hardwood	Total	Softwood	Hardwood
				standard cords			
1953	1,452,959	1,446,157	1,273,386	172,771	6,802	2,456	4,346
1954	1,341,209	1,330,888	1,160,479	170,409	10,321	7,016	3,305
1955	1,544,742	1,513,313	1,268,707	244,606	31,429	21,755	9,674
1956	1,845,299	1,806,571	1,582,860	223,711	38,728	26,443	12,285
1957	1,742,968	1,655,004	1,384,667	270,337	87,964	76,700	11,264
1958	1,747,779	1,592,643	1,346,288	246,355	155,136	134,959	20,177
1959	1,933,343	1,709,922	1,342,075	367,847	223,421	192,124	31,297
1960	2,190,439	1,901,857	1,515,038	386,819	288,582	238,981	49,601
1961	2,290,710	1,964,743	1,535,759	428,984	325,967	260,876	65,091
1962	2,481,455	2,091,988	1,615,196	476,792	389,467	307,749	81,718
1963	2,463,148	2,024,264	1,509,238	515,026	438,884	344,683	94,201
1964	2,629,617	2,164,989	1,657,783	507,206	464,628	375,710	88,918
1965	2,631,446	2,173,628	1,694,994	478,634	457,818	349,576	108,242
1966	2,854,328	2,343,512	1,803,443	540,069	510,816	366,321	144,495
1967	2,947,561	2,371,352	1,776,068	595,284	576,209	428,820	147,389
1968	2,897,329	2,371,915	1,724,356	647,559	525,414	393,276	132,138
1969	3,112,374	2,504,790	1,884,206	620,584	607,584	471,686	135,898
1970	3,300,745	2,557,589	2,009,093	548,496	743,156	568,272	174,884
1971	3,205,653	2,376,133	1,801,246	574,887	829,520	668,781	160,739
1972	3,473,921	2,547,590	1,990,989	556,601	926,331	750,918	175,413
1973	3,751,255	2,737,992	2,129,722	608,270	1,013,263	838,877	174,386
1974	3,842,880	2,781,465	2,154,268	627,197	1,061,415	854,810	206,605
1975	3,529,118	2,657,298	2,134,090	523,208	871,820	736,724	135,096
1976	3,880,439	2,601,535	2,009,860	591,675	1,278,904	1,030,111	248,793
1977	4,421,580	2,683,178	1,962,989	720,189	1,738,402	1,499,077	239,325
1978	4,306,979	2,680,477	1,934,353	746,124	1,626,502	1,352,218	274,284
1979	4,544,120	2,762,609	2,101,528	661,081	1,781,511	1,421,713	359,798
1980	4,296,594	2,765,808	2,135,054	630,754	1,530,786	1,244,508	286,278
1981	4,102,402	2,814,384	2,181,811	632,573	1,288,018	1,118,995	169,023
1982	4,077,253	2,857,229	2,169,305	687,924	1,220,024	1,062,313	157,711
1983	4,369,924	2,926,901	2,089,558	837,343	1,443,023	1,181,315	261,708
1984	4,472,846	3,170,650	2,147,442	1,023,208	1,302,196	1,053,483	248,713
1985	4,807,151	3,280,155	2,289,155	991,000	1,526,996	1,297,509	229,487
1986	4,814,606	3,211,697	2,175,506	1,036,191	1,602,909	1,427,927	174,982
1987	5,271,734	3,587,848	2,465,538	1,122,310	1,683,886	1,502,996	180,890
1988	5,141,071	3,671,220	2,535,522	1,135,698	1,469,851	1,274,914	194,937
1989	5,244,898	3,714,101	2,601,632	1,112,469	1,530,797	1,334,379	196,418
1990	5,220,892	3,763,600	2,763,362	1,000,238	1,457,292	1,282,175	175,117
1991	4,612,664	3,280,492	2,342,018	938,474	1,332,172	1,144,489	187,683
1992	5,410,307	3,878,307	2,764,733	1,113,574	1,532,000	1,346,086	185,914
1993	5,704,419	4,440,610	2,940,724	1,499,886	1,263,809	1,074,008	189,801
1994	5,989,356	4,555,505	3,202,505	1,353,000	1,433,851	1,219,978	213,873
1995	5,733,833	4,511,994	2,992,504	1,519,490	1,221,839	1,042,349	179,490
1996	5,591,443	4,191,416	2,695,629	1,495,787	1,400,027	1,209,752	190,275
1997	6,041,625	4,498,773	2,915,538	1,583,235	1,542,852	1,090,487	452,365
1998	5,691,814	4,281,135	2,850,949	1,430,186	1,410,679	1,188,729	221,950
1999	6,387,947	4,515,655	3,040,551	1,475,104	1,872,292	1,257,982	614,310
2000	5,671,480	3,849,486	2,773,957	1,075,529	1,821,994	1,358,996	462,998
2001	5,628,325	3,768,892	2,689,827	1,079,065	1,859,433	1,392,368	467,065
2002	5,816,023	3,819,390	2,786,556	1,032,834	1,996,633	1,476,339	520,294
2003	5,276,566	3,929,163	2,961,072	968,091	1,347,403	1,177,468	169,935
2004	5,746,254	4,314,274	3,108,297	1,205,977	1,431,980	1,227,558	204,422
2005	5,940,545	4,496,545	3,344,439	1,152,106	1,444,000	1,308,272	135,728
2006	6,052,113	4,386,378	3,253,286	1,133,092	1,665,735	1,442,386	223,349

Table A.14b—Trends in pulpwood production by species group, South Carolina, 1953 to 2006

Year	Total production	Roundwood Total	Softwood	Hardwood	Residues Total	Softwood	Hardwood
				green tons			
1953	3,938,521	3,921,901	3,438,142	483,759	16,620	5,907	10,713
1954	3,635,459	3,610,439	3,133,293	477,145	25,020	16,873	8,147
1955	4,186,573	4,110,406	3,425,509	684,897	76,167	52,321	23,846
1956	4,993,991	4,900,113	4,273,722	626,391	93,878	63,595	30,283
1957	4,707,774	4,495,545	3,738,601	756,944	212,229	184,464	27,766
1958	4,699,084	4,324,772	3,634,978	689,794	374,313	324,576	49,736
1959	5,192,779	4,653,574	3,623,603	1,029,972	539,205	462,058	77,147
1960	5,870,712	5,173,696	4,090,603	1,083,093	697,016	574,749	122,266
1961	6,135,561	5,347,705	4,146,549	1,201,155	787,856	627,407	160,449
1962	6,637,618	5,696,047	4,361,029	1,335,018	941,571	740,136	201,435
1963	6,578,183	5,517,015	4,074,943	1,442,073	1,061,168	828,963	232,205
1964	7,018,956	5,896,191	4,476,014	1,420,177	1,122,765	903,583	219,183
1965	7,024,206	5,916,659	4,576,484	1,340,175	1,107,547	840,730	266,817
1966	7,618,671	6,381,489	4,869,296	1,512,193	1,237,182	881,002	356,180
1967	7,856,805	6,462,179	4,795,384	1,666,795	1,394,626	1,031,312	363,314
1968	7,740,475	6,468,926	4,655,761	1,813,165	1,271,549	945,829	325,720
1969	8,294,385	6,824,991	5,087,356	1,737,635	1,469,393	1,134,405	334,989
1970	8,758,123	6,960,340	5,424,551	1,535,789	1,797,783	1,366,694	431,089
1971	8,477,688	6,473,048	4,863,364	1,609,684	2,004,640	1,608,418	396,222
1972	9,172,504	6,934,153	5,375,670	1,558,483	2,238,351	1,805,958	432,393
1973	9,900,766	7,453,405	5,750,249	1,703,156	2,447,361	2,017,499	429,861
1974	10,137,775	7,572,675	5,816,524	1,756,152	2,565,099	2,055,818	509,281
1975	9,331,858	7,227,025	5,762,043	1,464,982	2,104,833	1,771,821	333,012
1976	10,174,004	7,083,312	5,426,622	1,656,690	3,090,692	2,477,417	613,275
1977	11,511,816	7,316,600	5,300,070	2,016,529	4,195,216	3,605,280	589,936
1978	11,240,095	7,311,900	5,222,753	2,089,147	3,928,194	3,252,084	676,110
1979	11,831,274	7,525,152	5,674,126	1,851,027	4,306,122	3,419,220	886,902
1980	11,229,474	7,530,757	5,764,646	1,766,111	3,698,717	2,993,042	705,675
1981	10,769,919	7,662,094	5,890,890	1,771,204	3,107,825	2,691,183	416,642
1982	10,726,931	7,783,311	5,857,124	1,926,187	2,943,620	2,554,863	388,758
1983	11,472,540	7,986,367	5,641,807	2,344,560	3,486,173	2,841,063	645,110
1984	11,809,780	8,663,076	5,798,093	2,864,982	3,146,704	2,533,627	613,078
1985	12,641,713	8,955,519	6,180,719	2,774,800	3,686,195	3,120,509	565,685
1986	12,640,696	8,775,201	5,873,866	2,901,335	3,865,495	3,434,164	431,331
1987	13,860,020	9,799,421	6,656,953	3,142,468	4,060,599	3,614,705	445,894
1988	13,572,552	10,025,864	6,845,909	3,179,954	3,546,688	3,066,168	480,520
1989	13,832,671	10,139,320	7,024,406	3,114,913	3,693,352	3,209,181	484,170
1990	13,777,038	10,261,744	7,461,077	2,800,666	3,515,294	3,083,631	431,663
1991	12,166,310	8,951,176	6,323,449	2,627,727	3,215,135	2,752,496	462,639
1992	14,278,401	10,582,786	7,464,779	3,118,007	3,695,615	3,237,337	458,278
1993	15,190,484	12,139,636	7,939,955	4,199,681	3,050,849	2,582,989	467,859
1994	15,896,408	12,435,164	8,646,764	3,788,400	3,461,244	2,934,047	527,197
1995	15,283,625	12,334,333	8,079,761	4,254,572	2,949,292	2,506,849	442,443
1996	14,844,883	11,466,402	7,278,198	4,188,204	3,378,481	2,909,454	469,028
1997	16,042,712	12,305,011	7,871,953	4,433,058	3,737,701	2,622,621	1,115,080
1998	15,108,083	11,702,083	7,697,562	4,004,521	3,406,000	2,858,893	547,107
1999	16,879,500	12,339,779	8,209,488	4,130,291	4,539,721	3,025,447	1,514,274
2000	14,910,841	10,501,165	7,489,684	3,011,481	4,409,675	3,268,385	1,141,290
2001	14,783,875	10,283,915	7,262,533	3,021,382	4,499,960	3,348,645	1,151,315
2002	15,248,756	10,415,636	7,523,701	2,891,935	4,833,120	3,550,595	1,282,525
2003	13,956,250	10,705,549	7,994,894	2,710,655	3,250,700	2,831,811	418,890
2004	15,225,315	11,769,138	8,392,402	3,376,736	3,456,177	2,952,277	503,900
2005	15,736,846	12,255,882	9,029,985	3,225,897	3,480,964	3,146,394	334,570
2006	15,976,023	11,956,530	8,783,872	3,172,658	4,019,494	3,468,938	550,555

Table A.14c—Trends in pulpwood production by species group, South Carolina, 1953 to 2006

Year	Total production	Roundwood Total	Softwood	Hardwood	Residues Total	Softwood	Hardwood
				thousand cubic feet			
1953	114,087	113,595	99,688	13,907	491	172	319
1954	105,301	104,566	90,849	13,717	735	492	243
1955	121,247	119,011	99,322	19,689	2,235	1,525	711
1956	144,679	141,923	123,916	18,008	2,756	1,853	903
1957	149,203	143,000	117,100	25,900	6,203	5,376	828
1958	127,593	117,411	99,895	17,516	10,183	8,920	1,263
1959	140,393	125,736	99,582	26,154	14,657	12,698	1,959
1960	158,819	139,919	112,416	27,503	18,900	15,795	3,105
1961	165,771	144,454	113,953	30,501	21,316	17,242	4,074
1962	179,203	153,748	119,848	33,900	25,455	20,340	5,115
1963	177,282	148,604	111,985	36,619	28,678	22,781	5,896
1964	189,468	159,070	123,007	36,063	30,398	24,832	5,566
1965	189,679	159,800	125,769	34,031	29,880	23,105	6,775
1966	205,470	172,215	133,815	38,399	33,256	24,211	9,044
1967	211,677	174,109	131,784	42,325	37,568	28,342	9,226
1968	208,855	173,988	127,947	46,041	34,866	26,559	8,307
1969	224,329	183,931	139,808	44,123	40,398	31,854	8,544
1970	237,444	188,072	149,074	38,998	49,372	38,377	10,995
1971	229,758	174,488	133,634	40,854	55,270	45,165	10,106
1972	249,005	187,265	147,710	39,555	61,740	50,712	11,028
1973	268,844	201,229	158,007	43,222	67,615	56,652	10,964
1974	275,114	204,397	159,825	44,572	70,717	57,728	12,989
1975	253,751	195,505	158,327	37,178	58,246	49,753	8,493
1976	276,365	191,157	149,109	42,048	85,208	69,566	15,641
1977	347,290	231,007	177,786	53,221	116,283	101,237	15,046
1978	331,379	217,736	163,314	54,422	113,643	96,269	17,374
1979	344,961	220,954	166,766	54,188	124,007	101,217	22,791
1980	326,490	219,756	171,679	48,077	106,734	88,601	18,134
1981	323,830	233,459	186,830	46,629	90,371	79,665	10,706
1982	301,838	216,218	168,391	47,827	85,620	75,630	9,990
1983	323,471	222,792	164,913	57,879	100,679	84,102	16,577
1984	332,038	241,283	171,222	70,061	90,755	75,001	15,754
1985	344,125	237,215	169,481	67,734	106,910	92,374	14,536
1986	347,283	238,913	165,197	73,716	108,370	97,292	11,079
1987	386,493	272,634	193,216	79,418	113,859	102,406	11,453
1988	382,381	283,173	202,198	80,975	99,208	86,866	12,342
1989	382,382	279,029	200,144	78,885	103,353	90,918	12,436
1990	377,173	278,725	200,214	78,511	98,448	87,361	11,087
1991	339,518	249,656	183,394	66,262	89,862	77,980	11,883
1992	387,743	284,257	205,596	78,661	103,486	91,715	11,771
1993	405,639	324,633	218,683	105,949	81,007	69,171	11,836
1994	426,094	334,185	238,111	96,074	91,909	78,572	13,337
1995	397,843	319,518	211,577	107,941	78,325	67,132	11,193
1996	386,623	296,844	190,587	106,257	89,779	77,913	11,865
1997	420,003	321,562	209,515	112,047	98,441	70,232	28,208
1998	396,489	306,089	204,873	101,216	90,400	76,559	13,840
1999	442,943	323,616	219,352	104,264	119,327	81,020	38,307
2000	392,537	276,140	200,119	76,021	116,397	87,525	28,871
2001	386,464	269,788	193,408	76,380	116,676	87,551	29,124
2002	398,698	273,423	200,363	73,060	125,275	92,831	32,443
2003	358,259	273,624	205,321	68,303	84,635	74,039	10,596
2004	390,552	300,616	215,530	85,087	89,935	77,188	12,747
2005	408,463	317,736	236,513	81,223	90,727	82,263	8,463
2006	414,573	309,949	230,067	79,883	104,624	90,697	13,927

Table A.15a—Trends in pulpwood production by species group, Tennessee, 1953 to 2006

Year	Total production	Roundwood			Residues		
		Total	Softwood	Hardwood	Total	Softwood	Hardwood
				standard cords			
1953	235,260	234,162	105,345	128,817	1,098	397	701
1954	242,196	240,332	134,149	106,183	1,864	1,267	597
1955	333,418	326,634	220,805	105,829	6,784	4,696	2,088
1956	398,772	392,156	244,833	147,323	6,616	0	6,616
1957	341,194	334,287	236,111	98,176	6,907	0	6,907
1958	354,629	348,496	241,100	107,396	6,133	271	5,862
1959	352,988	346,077	200,818	145,259	6,911	665	6,246
1960	361,778	353,422	188,754	164,668	8,356	1,133	7,223
1961	418,465	403,790	214,771	189,019	14,675	4,093	10,582
1962	432,299	409,819	201,458	208,361	22,480	9,820	12,660
1963	426,767	395,843	198,662	197,181	30,924	10,621	20,303
1964	417,367	385,480	192,366	193,114	31,887	13,279	18,608
1965	415,936	384,640	184,334	200,306	31,296	10,113	21,183
1966	370,010	327,418	152,158	175,260	42,592	9,975	32,617
1967	395,158	336,504	157,646	178,858	58,654	8,681	49,973
1968	416,913	351,536	159,682	191,854	65,377	9,804	55,573
1969	430,277	364,703	167,890	196,813	65,574	12,788	52,786
1970	567,383	436,941	190,105	246,836	130,442	12,125	118,317
1971	629,722	475,702	195,794	279,908	154,020	12,833	141,187
1972	633,925	453,224	180,791	272,433	180,701	14,822	165,879
1973	681,442	440,604	163,772	276,832	240,838	49,013	191,825
1974	818,906	521,319	229,891	291,428	297,587	23,905	273,682
1975	743,199	561,781	209,446	352,335	181,418	17,797	163,621
1976	758,525	525,216	229,717	295,499	233,309	23,517	209,792
1977	670,589	470,898	213,884	257,014	199,691	17,895	181,796
1978	687,967	466,446	203,936	262,510	221,521	40,207	181,314
1979	955,429	647,018	228,799	418,219	308,411	26,213	282,198
1980	1,235,963	783,185	354,362	428,823	452,778	66,984	385,794
1981	1,344,474	822,742	405,449	417,293	521,732	53,719	468,013
1982	897,230	570,729	169,733	400,996	326,501	70,187	256,314
1983	1,419,520	1,016,019	512,409	503,610	403,501	19,908	383,593
1984	1,368,188	999,962	530,486	469,476	368,226	32,918	335,308
1985	1,239,699	881,998	505,964	376,034	357,701	39,828	317,873
1986	1,478,863	1,227,830	788,945	438,885	251,033	47,626	203,407
1987	1,353,675	1,020,062	615,068	404,994	333,613	42,427	291,186
1988	1,221,644	960,204	573,872	386,332	261,440	44,118	217,322
1989	1,224,049	997,470	600,659	396,811	226,579	32,892	193,687
1990	1,430,074	1,100,658	716,394	384,264	329,416	53,192	276,224
1991	1,446,038	1,150,328	743,200	407,128	295,710	56,792	238,918
1992	1,337,016	1,027,919	564,503	463,416	309,097	158,295	150,802
1993	1,376,717	1,138,403	599,806	538,597	238,314	29,395	208,919
1994	1,586,154	1,363,500	628,200	735,300	222,654	23,168	199,486
1995	1,762,178	1,459,555	617,927	841,628	302,623	45,983	256,640
1996	1,787,124	1,519,924	682,199	837,725	267,200	29,101	238,099
1997	1,907,330	1,624,565	700,255	924,310	282,765	45,645	237,120
1998	1,851,128	1,576,778	701,971	874,807	274,350	24,404	249,946
1999	1,921,590	1,619,507	719,116	900,391	302,083	25,449	276,634
2000	2,117,663	1,776,502	836,992	939,510	341,161	47,166	293,995
2001	1,966,662	1,700,307	760,425	939,882	266,355	45,452	220,903
2002	1,845,108	1,550,032	564,408	985,624	295,076	41,208	253,868
2003	1,931,227	1,616,512	634,409	982,103	314,715	15,122	299,593
2004	1,837,871	1,482,893	542,332	940,561	354,978	14,879	340,099
2005	1,983,721	1,611,937	551,616	1,060,321	371,784	14,947	356,837
2006	1,944,909	1,578,130	579,135	998,995	366,779	17,678	349,101

Table A.15b—Trends in pulpwood production by species group, Tennessee, 1953 to 2006

Year	Total production	Roundwood			Residues		
		Total	Softwood	Hardwood	Total	Softwood	Hardwood
				green tons			
1953	647,802	645,119	284,432	360,688	2,683	955	1,728
1954	664,033	659,515	362,202	297,312	4,519	3,047	1,472
1955	908,936	892,495	596,174	296,321	16,441	11,294	5,147
1956	1,089,862	1,073,554	661,049	412,504	16,308	0	16,308
1957	929,418	912,393	637,500	274,893	17,026	0	17,026
1958	966,780	951,679	650,970	300,709	15,102	652	14,450
1959	965,930	948,934	542,209	406,725	16,996	1,599	15,396
1960	991,236	970,706	509,636	461,070	20,530	2,725	17,805
1961	1,145,063	1,109,135	579,882	529,253	35,928	9,844	26,085
1962	1,182,171	1,127,347	543,937	583,411	54,824	23,617	31,207
1963	1,164,085	1,088,494	536,387	552,107	75,590	25,544	50,047
1964	1,137,912	1,060,107	519,388	540,719	77,805	31,936	45,869
1965	1,135,096	1,058,559	497,702	560,857	76,538	24,322	52,216
1966	1,005,945	901,555	410,827	490,728	104,391	23,990	80,401
1967	1,070,508	926,447	425,644	500,802	144,061	20,878	123,183
1968	1,128,899	968,333	431,141	537,191	160,566	23,579	136,987
1969	1,165,252	1,004,379	453,303	551,076	160,873	30,755	130,117
1970	1,525,236	1,204,424	513,284	691,141	320,812	29,161	291,651
1971	1,691,276	1,312,386	528,644	783,742	378,889	30,863	348,026
1972	1,695,487	1,250,948	488,136	762,812	444,539	35,647	408,892
1973	1,808,039	1,217,314	442,184	775,130	590,725	117,876	472,849
1974	2,168,822	1,436,704	620,706	815,998	732,118	57,492	674,626
1975	1,998,170	1,552,042	565,504	986,538	446,128	42,802	403,326
1976	2,021,329	1,447,633	620,236	827,397	573,696	56,558	517,137
1977	1,788,291	1,297,126	577,487	719,639	491,165	43,037	448,127
1978	1,829,292	1,285,655	550,627	735,028	543,637	96,698	446,939
1979	2,547,431	1,788,771	617,757	1,171,013	758,660	63,042	695,618
1980	3,269,561	2,157,482	956,777	1,200,704	1,112,079	161,097	950,982
1981	3,545,979	2,263,133	1,094,712	1,168,420	1,282,846	129,194	1,153,652
1982	2,381,682	1,581,068	458,279	1,122,789	800,614	168,800	631,814
1983	3,787,048	2,793,612	1,383,504	1,410,108	993,435	47,879	945,557
1984	3,652,547	2,746,845	1,432,312	1,314,533	905,702	79,168	826,534
1985	3,298,341	2,418,998	1,366,103	1,052,895	879,343	95,786	783,557
1986	3,974,968	3,359,030	2,130,152	1,228,878	615,939	114,541	501,398
1987	3,614,477	2,794,667	1,660,684	1,133,983	819,810	102,037	717,773
1988	3,272,987	2,631,184	1,549,454	1,081,730	641,803	106,104	535,699
1989	3,289,394	2,732,850	1,621,779	1,111,071	556,544	79,105	477,438
1990	3,819,022	3,010,203	1,934,264	1,075,939	808,819	127,927	680,892
1991	3,872,116	3,146,598	2,006,640	1,139,958	725,518	136,585	588,933
1992	3,574,149	2,821,723	1,524,158	1,297,565	752,426	380,699	371,727
1993	3,713,228	3,127,548	1,619,476	1,508,072	585,680	70,695	514,985
1994	4,302,432	3,754,980	1,696,140	2,058,840	547,452	55,719	491,733
1995	4,768,168	4,024,961	1,668,403	2,356,558	743,207	110,589	632,618
1996	4,844,469	4,187,567	1,841,937	2,345,630	656,902	69,988	586,914
1997	5,173,034	4,478,757	1,890,689	2,588,068	694,277	109,776	584,501
1998	5,019,590	4,344,781	1,895,322	2,449,460	674,809	58,692	616,117
1999	5,205,816	4,462,708	1,941,613	2,521,095	743,108	61,205	681,903
2000	5,728,638	4,890,506	2,259,878	2,630,628	838,132	113,434	724,698
2001	5,338,655	4,684,817	2,053,148	2,631,670	653,838	109,312	544,526
2002	5,008,539	4,283,649	1,523,902	2,759,747	724,890	99,105	625,785
2003	5,237,658	4,462,793	1,712,904	2,749,888	774,865	36,368	738,497
2004	4,971,995	4,097,867	1,464,296	2,633,571	874,128	35,784	838,344
2005	5,373,813	4,458,262	1,489,363	2,968,899	915,551	35,948	879,603
2006	5,263,900	4,360,851	1,563,665	2,797,186	903,050	42,516	860,534

Table A.15c—Trends in pulpwood production by species group, Tennessee, 1953 to 2006

Year	Total production	Roundwood			Residues		
		Total	Softwood	Hardwood	Total	Softwood	Hardwood
		thousand cubic feet					
1953	18,039	17,965	7,943	10,022	75	27	48
1954	18,502	18,376	10,115	8,261	126	85	41
1955	25,340	24,882	16,649	8,233	458	315	143
1956	30,375	29,922	18,460	11,462	453	0	453
1957	25,914	25,441	17,803	7,638	473	0	473
1958	26,954	26,534	18,179	8,355	420	18	401
1959	26,915	26,443	15,142	11,301	472	45	428
1960	27,614	27,043	14,232	12,811	571	76	495
1961	33,558	32,517	17,396	15,122	1,041	295	745
1962	34,586	32,986	16,317	16,669	1,600	708	892
1963	34,062	31,866	16,091	15,774	2,196	766	1,430
1964	33,299	31,030	15,581	15,449	2,269	958	1,311
1965	33,176	30,955	14,931	16,024	2,222	730	1,492
1966	29,362	26,345	12,324	14,021	3,017	720	2,297
1967	31,223	27,077	12,769	14,309	4,146	626	3,520
1968	32,903	28,282	12,934	15,348	4,621	707	3,914
1969	33,984	29,344	13,599	15,745	4,640	923	3,718
1970	44,353	35,145	15,398	19,747	9,208	875	8,333
1971	49,121	38,252	15,859	22,393	10,869	926	9,944
1972	49,191	36,439	14,644	21,795	12,752	1,069	11,683
1973	52,458	35,412	13,266	22,147	17,046	3,536	13,510
1974	62,935	41,935	18,621	23,314	21,000	1,725	19,275
1975	57,960	45,152	16,965	28,187	12,808	1,284	11,524
1976	58,719	42,247	18,607	23,640	16,472	1,697	14,775
1977	51,980	37,886	17,325	20,561	14,095	1,291	12,804
1978	53,190	37,520	16,519	21,001	15,671	2,901	12,770
1979	73,756	51,990	18,533	33,458	21,766	1,891	19,875
1980	90,785	59,848	26,400	33,448	30,937	4,445	26,492
1981	98,457	62,755	30,206	32,549	35,702	3,565	32,137
1982	66,181	43,923	12,645	31,278	22,258	4,658	17,601
1983	105,118	77,456	38,174	39,282	27,662	1,321	26,341
1984	101,350	76,140	39,521	36,619	25,209	2,184	23,025
1985	91,496	67,025	37,694	29,331	24,471	2,643	21,828
1986	110,137	93,009	58,776	34,233	17,128	3,160	13,968
1987	100,223	77,412	45,823	31,590	22,811	2,815	19,995
1988	90,738	72,887	42,753	30,134	17,851	2,928	14,923
1989	89,593	74,416	43,585	30,831	15,177	2,126	13,051
1990	103,455	81,405	51,983	29,422	22,050	3,438	18,612
1991	104,869	85,100	53,928	31,172	19,769	3,671	16,098
1992	96,836	76,443	40,961	35,482	20,393	10,231	10,161
1993	100,738	84,761	43,523	41,238	15,977	1,900	14,077
1994	116,821	101,882	45,583	56,299	14,939	1,497	13,442
1995	129,543	109,278	44,838	64,440	20,265	2,972	17,293
1996	131,567	113,643	49,502	64,141	17,924	1,881	16,043
1997	140,509	121,581	50,813	70,768	18,928	2,950	15,977
1998	136,248	117,829	50,936	66,893	18,419	1,577	16,842
1999	141,408	121,117	52,185	68,932	20,291	1,645	18,646
2000	155,531	132,666	60,739	71,927	22,865	3,049	19,816
2001	144,971	127,144	55,183	71,961	17,828	2,938	14,890
2002	136,197	116,421	40,958	75,463	19,775	2,663	17,112
2003	142,400	121,229	46,031	75,198	21,171	977	20,194
2004	135,253	111,367	39,351	72,017	23,886	962	22,924
2005	146,226	121,208	40,018	81,190	25,018	966	24,052
2006	143,182	118,509	42,015	76,494	24,673	1,143	23,531

Table A.16a—Trends in pulpwood production by species group, Texas, 1953 to 2006

Year	Total production	Roundwood Total	Roundwood Softwood	Roundwood Hardwood	Residues Total	Residues Softwood	Residues Hardwood
				standard cords			
1953	1,216,382	1,210,704	1,159,261	51,443	5,678	2,050	3,628
1954	1,062,509	1,054,333	1,003,561	50,772	8,176	5,558	2,618
1955	1,228,775	1,203,775	1,119,486	84,289	25,000	17,305	7,695
1956	1,552,494	1,459,015	1,339,239	119,776	93,479	93,138	341
1957	1,421,346	1,226,218	1,065,690	160,528	195,128	194,757	371
1958	1,385,972	1,126,886	954,014	172,872	259,086	254,333	4,753
1959	1,415,639	1,120,048	906,329	213,719	295,591	279,012	16,579
1960	1,426,377	1,134,517	916,547	217,970	291,860	276,111	15,749
1961	1,441,561	1,130,494	906,932	223,562	311,067	288,813	22,254
1962	1,429,593	1,091,414	838,192	253,222	338,179	324,726	13,453
1963	1,443,586	1,062,974	820,319	242,655	380,612	352,208	28,404
1964	1,590,486	1,144,376	857,376	287,000	446,110	404,018	42,092
1965	1,669,003	1,156,161	789,877	366,284	512,842	467,513	45,329
1966	1,904,126	1,374,713	975,069	399,644	529,413	491,590	37,823
1967	1,993,132	1,409,935	1,087,303	322,632	583,197	538,103	45,094
1968	2,520,010	1,818,602	1,507,513	311,089	701,408	668,226	33,182
1969	2,834,057	2,008,023	1,654,502	353,521	826,034	785,623	40,411
1970	2,917,598	2,092,598	1,819,711	272,887	825,000	758,096	66,904
1971	3,129,392	2,177,208	1,883,864	293,344	952,184	880,676	71,508
1972	3,323,130	2,198,635	1,836,124	362,511	1,124,495	1,064,588	59,907
1973	3,612,723	2,373,626	1,985,799	387,827	1,239,097	1,070,514	168,583
1974	3,847,304	2,601,285	2,168,435	432,850	1,246,019	1,125,804	120,215
1975	3,626,821	2,408,546	2,114,933	293,613	1,218,275	1,093,285	124,990
1976	3,801,280	2,405,456	2,004,780	400,676	1,395,824	1,269,505	126,319
1977	3,741,843	2,340,269	1,944,322	395,947	1,401,574	1,240,786	160,788
1978	4,032,645	2,661,238	2,179,476	481,762	1,371,407	1,211,890	159,517
1979	3,890,263	2,504,252	2,057,006	447,246	1,386,011	1,244,913	141,098
1980	4,195,216	2,865,831	2,393,985	471,846	1,329,385	1,153,587	175,798
1981	4,080,805	2,426,025	2,041,319	384,706	1,654,780	1,415,992	238,788
1982	3,917,224	2,391,528	1,892,059	499,469	1,525,696	1,411,578	114,118
1983	4,230,604	2,442,769	1,706,636	736,133	1,787,835	1,645,722	142,113
1984	4,274,339	2,440,373	1,739,345	701,028	1,833,966	1,633,284	200,682
1985	4,135,648	2,129,306	1,573,256	556,050	2,006,342	1,630,321	376,021
1986	3,770,524	2,070,196	1,443,992	626,204	1,700,328	1,315,324	385,004
1987	4,035,159	1,947,878	1,518,051	429,827	2,087,281	1,438,989	648,292
1988	4,056,858	2,122,412	1,718,022	404,390	1,934,446	1,272,317	662,129
1989	4,389,501	2,455,015	1,777,088	677,927	1,934,486	1,513,906	420,580
1990	4,296,301	2,369,390	1,905,881	463,509	1,926,911	1,306,581	620,330
1991	4,431,334	2,360,073	1,899,337	460,736	2,071,261	1,499,979	571,282
1992	4,533,994	2,516,941	2,007,554	509,387	2,017,053	1,480,824	536,229
1993	4,234,164	2,324,679	1,827,110	497,569	1,909,485	1,382,611	526,874
1994	4,306,845	2,041,960	1,565,403	476,557	2,264,885	1,682,491	582,394
1995	5,124,458	2,713,906	1,874,061	839,845	2,410,552	1,725,653	684,899
1996	4,483,612	2,325,797	1,650,745	675,052	2,157,815	1,540,767	617,048
1997	4,984,811	3,867,588	2,441,638	1,425,950	1,117,223	1,048,534	68,689
1998	4,584,866	2,680,950	1,922,693	758,257	1,903,916	1,452,438	451,478
1999	3,960,647	2,202,076	1,472,009	730,067	1,758,571	1,295,027	463,544
2000	3,283,062	1,531,577	934,795	596,782	1,751,485	1,297,952	453,533
2001	3,124,407	2,125,414	1,080,691	1,044,723	998,993	866,475	132,518
2002	2,957,993	2,083,171	1,123,618	959,553	874,822	763,299	111,523
2003	3,504,243	2,601,652	1,601,588	1,000,064	902,591	797,840	104,751
2004	3,418,703	2,671,572	1,549,746	1,121,826	747,131	590,609	156,522
2005	3,358,362	2,617,595	1,501,816	1,115,779	740,767	634,221	106,546
2006	3,125,073	2,258,996	1,236,835	1,022,161	866,077	736,695	129,382

Table A.16b—Trends in pulpwood production by species group, Texas, 1953 to 2006

Year	Total production	Roundwood Total	Roundwood Softwood	Roundwood Hardwood	Residues Total	Residues Softwood	Residues Hardwood
				green tons			
1953	3,287,918	3,274,045	3,130,005	144,040	13,873	4,930	8,943
1954	2,871,597	2,851,776	2,709,615	142,162	19,820	13,367	6,453
1955	3,319,208	3,258,621	3,022,612	236,009	60,587	41,619	18,968
1956	4,176,156	3,951,318	3,615,945	335,373	224,837	223,997	841
1957	3,796,147	3,326,841	2,877,363	449,478	469,305	468,391	915
1958	3,683,266	3,059,879	2,575,838	484,042	623,387	611,671	11,716
1959	3,757,393	3,045,502	2,447,088	598,413	711,891	671,024	40,867
1960	3,787,861	3,084,993	2,474,677	610,316	702,868	664,047	38,821
1961	3,824,141	3,074,690	2,448,716	625,974	749,451	694,595	54,856
1962	3,786,268	2,972,140	2,263,118	709,022	814,128	780,966	33,162
1963	3,811,371	2,894,295	2,214,861	679,434	917,076	847,060	70,016
1964	4,193,935	3,118,515	2,314,915	803,600	1,075,420	971,663	103,757
1965	4,394,368	3,158,263	2,132,668	1,025,595	1,236,105	1,124,369	111,736
1966	5,027,197	3,751,690	2,632,686	1,119,003	1,275,508	1,182,274	93,234
1967	5,244,382	3,839,088	2,935,718	903,370	1,405,294	1,294,138	111,157
1968	6,630,211	4,941,334	4,070,285	871,049	1,688,877	1,607,084	81,794
1969	7,446,051	5,457,014	4,467,155	989,859	1,989,036	1,889,423	99,613
1970	7,665,443	5,677,303	4,913,220	764,084	1,988,139	1,823,221	164,918
1971	8,202,089	5,907,796	5,086,433	821,363	2,294,293	2,118,026	176,267
1972	8,680,570	5,972,566	4,957,535	1,015,031	2,708,005	2,560,334	147,671
1973	9,437,716	6,447,573	5,361,657	1,085,916	2,990,143	2,574,586	415,557
1974	10,070,643	7,066,755	5,854,775	1,211,980	3,003,889	2,707,559	296,330
1975	9,469,886	6,532,436	5,710,319	822,116	2,937,451	2,629,350	308,100
1976	9,899,335	6,534,799	5,412,906	1,121,893	3,364,536	3,053,160	311,376
1977	9,738,754	6,358,321	5,249,669	1,108,652	3,380,433	2,984,090	396,342
1978	10,541,324	7,233,519	5,884,585	1,348,934	3,307,805	2,914,595	393,209
1979	10,148,027	6,806,205	5,553,916	1,252,289	3,341,822	2,994,016	347,807
1980	10,992,647	7,784,928	6,463,760	1,321,169	3,207,719	2,774,377	433,342
1981	10,582,811	6,588,738	5,511,561	1,077,177	3,994,073	3,405,461	588,612
1982	10,183,218	6,507,073	5,108,559	1,398,513	3,676,146	3,394,845	281,301
1983	10,977,360	6,669,090	4,607,917	2,061,172	4,308,270	3,957,961	350,309
1984	11,081,839	6,659,110	4,696,232	1,962,878	4,422,729	3,928,048	494,681
1985	10,652,545	5,804,731	4,247,791	1,556,940	4,847,814	3,920,922	926,892
1986	9,764,539	5,652,150	3,898,778	1,753,371	4,112,389	3,163,354	949,035
1987	10,361,062	5,302,253	4,098,738	1,203,516	5,058,808	3,460,769	1,598,040
1988	10,463,022	5,770,951	4,638,659	1,132,292	4,692,070	3,059,922	1,632,148
1989	11,374,007	6,696,333	4,798,138	1,898,196	4,677,674	3,640,944	1,036,730
1990	11,115,145	6,443,704	5,145,879	1,297,825	4,671,441	3,142,327	1,529,113
1991	11,433,930	6,418,271	5,128,210	1,290,061	5,015,660	3,607,449	1,408,210
1992	11,729,866	6,846,679	5,420,396	1,426,284	4,883,186	3,561,382	1,321,804
1993	10,950,314	6,326,390	4,933,197	1,393,193	4,623,924	3,325,179	1,298,744
1994	11,042,940	5,560,948	4,226,588	1,334,360	5,481,992	4,046,391	1,435,601
1995	13,250,002	7,411,531	5,059,965	2,351,566	5,838,472	4,150,195	1,688,276
1996	11,573,725	6,347,157	4,457,012	1,890,146	5,226,568	3,705,545	1,521,023
1997	13,276,125	10,585,083	6,592,423	3,992,660	2,691,043	2,521,724	169,318
1998	11,920,397	7,314,391	5,191,271	2,123,120	4,606,007	3,493,113	1,112,893
1999	10,275,788	6,018,612	3,974,424	2,044,188	4,257,176	3,114,540	1,142,636
2000	8,434,470	4,194,936	2,523,947	1,670,990	4,239,533	3,121,575	1,117,959
2001	8,253,619	5,843,090	2,917,866	2,925,224	2,410,529	2,083,872	326,657
2002	7,831,155	5,720,517	3,033,769	2,686,748	2,110,638	1,835,734	274,904
2003	9,301,483	7,124,467	4,324,288	2,800,179	2,177,016	1,918,805	258,211
2004	9,131,668	7,325,427	4,184,314	3,141,113	1,806,241	1,420,415	385,827
2005	8,967,022	7,179,084	4,054,903	3,124,181	1,787,937	1,525,302	262,636
2006	8,292,183	6,201,505	3,339,455	2,862,051	2,090,678	1,771,751	318,927

Table A.16c—Trends in pulpwood production by species group, Texas, 1953 to 2006

Year	Total production	Roundwood Total	Softwood	Hardwood	Residues Total	Softwood	Hardwood
				thousand cubic feet			
1953	91,814	91,434	87,524	3,910	381	138	243
1954	80,176	79,628	75,769	3,859	549	374	175
1955	92,606	90,927	84,521	6,406	1,679	1,164	515
1956	116,502	110,216	101,113	9,103	6,286	6,264	23
1957	105,782	92,660	80,460	12,200	13,122	13,098	25
1958	102,588	85,166	72,028	13,138	17,422	17,104	318
1959	104,544	84,670	68,428	16,243	19,873	18,764	1,109
1960	105,387	85,765	69,199	16,566	19,622	18,569	1,054
1961	106,376	85,464	68,473	16,991	20,912	19,423	1,489
1962	105,267	82,528	63,283	19,245	22,738	21,838	900
1963	105,963	80,376	61,934	18,442	25,587	23,686	1,900
1964	124,522	92,407	69,447	22,960	32,114	29,150	2,964
1965	130,206	93,283	63,980	29,303	36,924	33,731	3,192
1966	149,084	110,952	78,981	31,972	38,132	35,468	2,664
1967	155,882	113,882	88,072	25,811	42,000	38,824	3,176
1968	197,545	146,996	122,109	24,887	50,549	48,213	2,337
1969	221,825	162,296	134,015	28,282	59,529	56,683	2,846
1970	228,636	169,228	147,397	21,831	59,409	54,697	4,712
1971	244,637	176,061	152,593	23,468	68,577	63,541	5,036
1972	258,756	177,727	148,726	29,001	81,029	76,810	4,219
1973	280,987	191,876	160,850	31,026	89,111	77,238	11,873
1974	299,965	210,271	175,643	34,628	89,693	81,227	8,467
1975	269,320	185,752	162,850	22,902	83,568	74,985	8,583
1976	281,366	185,621	154,368	31,253	95,746	87,072	8,674
1977	276,739	180,597	149,713	30,884	96,143	85,102	11,041
1978	299,471	205,397	167,820	37,577	94,074	83,120	10,954
1979	288,348	193,275	158,389	34,885	95,074	85,385	9,689
1980	312,334	221,141	184,337	36,804	91,193	79,121	12,072
1981	300,704	187,189	157,182	30,007	113,516	97,119	16,397
1982	289,299	184,647	145,689	38,959	104,652	96,816	7,836
1983	311,463	188,829	131,411	57,418	122,634	112,875	9,759
1984	314,412	188,610	133,930	54,680	125,803	112,022	13,780
1985	302,152	164,513	121,141	43,372	137,639	111,819	25,821
1986	270,487	156,517	108,299	48,218	113,969	87,871	26,098
1987	287,029	146,951	113,854	33,097	140,079	96,132	43,946
1988	289,872	159,990	128,852	31,138	129,882	84,998	44,884
1989	315,129	185,482	133,282	52,200	129,647	101,137	28,510
1990	307,969	178,631	142,941	35,690	129,337	87,287	42,051
1991	316,860	177,927	142,450	35,477	138,933	100,207	38,726
1992	322,912	188,531	149,563	38,968	134,381	98,268	36,114
1993	301,418	174,184	136,120	38,064	127,234	91,750	35,484
1994	303,952	153,079	116,623	36,457	150,873	111,650	39,223
1995	364,506	203,866	139,618	64,248	160,641	114,515	46,126
1996	318,424	174,622	122,981	51,641	143,802	102,246	41,557
1997	365,194	290,987	181,902	109,085	74,207	69,581	4,626
1998	328,037	201,247	143,241	58,007	126,790	96,384	30,406
1999	282,671	165,515	109,665	55,850	117,157	85,938	31,218
2000	231,973	115,296	69,642	45,654	116,677	86,132	30,544
2001	226,857	160,433	80,511	79,921	66,424	57,499	8,925
2002	215,279	157,115	83,710	73,406	58,163	50,653	7,511
2003	255,823	195,823	119,318	76,505	60,000	52,945	7,055
2004	251,010	201,276	115,456	85,820	49,734	39,193	10,541
2005	246,505	197,242	111,885	85,357	49,263	42,087	7,176
2006	227,940	170,340	92,144	78,195	57,601	48,887	8,714

Table A.17a—Trends in pulpwood production by species group, Virginia, 1953 to 2006

Year	Total production	Roundwood			Residues		
		Total	Softwood	Hardwood	Total	Softwood	Hardwood
				standard cords			
1953	1,273,308	1,267,347	1,033,601	233,746	5,961	2,152	3,809
1954	1,268,137	1,258,379	1,033,632	224,747	9,758	6,633	3,125
1955	1,435,527	1,406,320	1,138,078	268,242	29,207	20,217	8,990
1956	1,656,307	1,629,706	1,273,204	356,502	26,601	22,443	4,158
1957	1,518,431	1,418,272	1,080,181	338,091	100,159	97,028	3,131
1958	1,449,809	1,377,693	981,739	395,954	72,116	67,009	5,107
1959	1,728,364	1,643,828	1,241,806	402,022	84,536	73,831	10,705
1960	1,833,378	1,715,314	1,277,780	437,534	118,064	105,058	13,006
1961	1,833,700	1,662,209	1,190,021	472,188	171,491	153,664	17,827
1962	1,894,055	1,685,935	1,159,486	526,449	208,120	165,273	42,847
1963	1,990,067	1,771,957	1,235,469	536,488	218,110	165,199	52,911
1964	2,130,145	1,883,821	1,273,618	610,203	246,324	181,521	64,803
1965	2,420,896	2,094,146	1,423,972	670,174	326,750	226,880	99,870
1966	2,365,417	2,007,536	1,334,271	673,265	357,881	217,697	140,184
1967	2,358,961	1,898,921	1,230,871	668,050	460,040	264,545	195,495
1968	2,371,979	1,726,522	1,054,966	671,556	645,457	438,268	207,189
1969	2,409,799	1,830,217	996,373	833,844	579,582	391,677	187,905
1970	2,403,291	1,862,036	962,129	899,907	541,255	326,479	214,776
1971	2,300,891	1,711,911	873,820	838,091	588,980	351,791	237,189
1972	2,206,546	1,674,568	827,683	846,885	531,978	293,395	238,583
1973	2,551,359	1,778,694	844,632	934,062	772,665	437,273	335,392
1974	2,631,821	1,714,555	875,221	839,334	917,266	463,581	453,685
1975	2,336,436	1,428,865	721,771	707,094	907,571	553,394	354,177
1976	2,661,736	1,736,077	811,310	924,767	925,659	554,778	370,881
1977	2,637,859	1,680,249	825,658	854,591	957,610	588,119	369,491
1978	2,629,257	1,768,460	889,567	878,893	860,797	440,614	420,183
1979	2,666,759	1,638,548	891,856	746,692	1,028,211	486,713	541,498
1980	3,017,326	2,048,341	1,064,883	983,458	968,985	519,805	449,180
1981	3,163,288	2,254,287	1,042,783	1,211,504	909,001	510,489	398,512
1982	3,260,515	2,291,486	1,133,441	1,158,045	969,029	520,022	449,007
1983	3,499,791	2,551,025	1,124,839	1,426,186	948,766	467,278	481,488
1984	3,612,676	2,550,077	1,293,253	1,256,824	1,062,599	496,894	565,705
1985	3,537,390	2,278,978	1,062,972	1,216,006	1,258,412	709,701	548,711
1986	3,625,300	2,435,025	1,076,046	1,358,979	1,190,275	664,295	525,980
1987	3,016,472	1,854,477	904,951	949,526	1,161,995	737,694	424,301
1988	3,239,026	2,049,398	1,021,306	1,028,092	1,189,628	741,806	447,822
1989	3,416,314	2,219,411	1,164,520	1,054,891	1,196,903	741,178	455,725
1990	3,647,261	2,415,037	1,265,241	1,149,796	1,232,224	761,307	470,917
1991	3,407,249	2,306,956	1,235,355	1,071,601	1,100,293	684,981	415,312
1992	3,478,827	2,406,519	1,333,330	1,073,189	1,072,308	637,619	434,689
1993	3,582,975	2,553,073	1,478,077	1,074,996	1,029,902	686,896	343,006
1994	3,979,830	2,614,406	1,585,532	1,028,874	1,365,424	934,713	430,711
1995	3,713,895	2,643,284	1,511,737	1,131,547	1,070,611	598,927	471,684
1996	3,509,908	2,611,120	1,510,186	1,100,934	898,788	485,692	413,096
1997	4,053,150	2,889,592	1,641,198	1,248,394	1,163,558	738,742	424,816
1998	4,067,066	2,904,814	1,638,956	1,265,858	1,162,252	628,974	533,278
1999	3,612,457	2,301,920	1,301,138	1,000,782	1,310,537	655,070	655,467
2000	3,570,292	2,391,428	1,246,514	1,144,914	1,178,864	540,819	638,045
2001	3,513,525	2,248,207	1,193,463	1,054,744	1,265,318	594,886	670,432
2002	3,307,102	2,092,379	1,022,926	1,069,453	1,214,723	616,269	598,454
2003	3,440,870	2,457,910	1,186,281	1,271,629	982,960	532,620	450,340
2004	3,812,895	2,698,550	1,310,098	1,388,452	1,114,345	581,152	533,193
2005	4,194,608	2,637,110	1,285,800	1,351,310	1,557,498	827,922	729,576
2006	4,078,344	2,490,735	1,220,466	1,270,269	1,587,609	807,143	780,466

Table A.17b—Trends in pulpwood production by species group, Virginia, 1953 to 2006

Year	Total production	Roundwood Total	Softwood	Hardwood	Residues Total	Softwood	Hardwood
				green tons			
1953	3,459,776	3,445,212	2,790,723	654,489	14,565	5,176	9,389
1954	3,443,753	3,420,098	2,790,806	629,292	23,655	15,952	7,703
1955	3,894,670	3,823,888	3,072,811	751,078	70,782	48,622	22,160
1956	4,500,081	4,435,856	3,437,651	998,206	64,225	53,975	10,249
1957	4,104,214	3,863,144	2,916,489	946,655	241,070	233,352	7,718
1958	3,933,112	3,759,367	2,650,695	1,108,671	173,745	161,157	12,589
1959	4,682,489	4,478,538	3,352,876	1,125,662	203,951	177,564	26,388
1960	4,959,825	4,675,101	3,450,006	1,225,095	284,724	252,664	32,060
1961	4,948,689	4,535,183	3,213,057	1,322,126	413,505	369,562	43,944
1962	5,107,769	4,604,669	3,130,612	1,474,057	503,099	397,482	105,618
1963	5,365,662	4,837,933	3,335,766	1,502,166	527,729	397,304	130,426
1964	5,743,634	5,147,337	3,438,769	1,708,568	596,297	436,558	159,739
1965	6,513,038	5,721,212	3,844,724	1,876,487	791,826	545,646	246,180
1966	6,356,789	5,487,674	3,602,532	1,885,142	869,115	523,561	345,554
1967	6,312,018	5,193,892	3,323,352	1,870,540	1,118,126	636,231	481,895
1968	6,293,520	4,728,765	2,848,408	1,880,357	1,564,755	1,054,035	510,721
1969	6,430,139	5,024,970	2,690,207	2,334,763	1,405,169	941,983	463,186
1970	6,432,093	5,117,488	2,597,748	2,519,740	1,314,605	785,182	529,423
1971	6,136,697	4,705,969	2,359,314	2,346,655	1,430,728	846,057	584,671
1972	5,899,744	4,606,022	2,234,744	2,371,278	1,293,722	705,615	588,107
1973	6,774,263	4,895,880	2,280,506	2,615,374	1,878,383	1,051,642	826,741
1974	6,946,478	4,713,232	2,363,097	2,350,135	2,233,246	1,114,912	1,118,334
1975	6,132,604	3,928,645	1,948,782	1,979,863	2,203,959	1,330,913	873,046
1976	7,028,347	4,779,885	2,190,537	2,589,348	2,248,463	1,334,241	914,222
1977	6,947,353	4,622,131	2,229,277	2,392,855	2,325,222	1,414,426	910,795
1978	6,958,159	4,862,731	2,401,831	2,460,900	2,095,428	1,059,677	1,035,751
1979	7,004,086	4,498,749	2,408,011	2,090,738	2,505,337	1,170,545	1,334,793
1980	7,986,226	5,628,867	2,875,184	2,753,682	2,357,360	1,250,131	1,107,229
1981	8,417,783	6,207,725	2,815,514	3,392,211	2,210,058	1,227,726	982,332
1982	8,660,272	6,302,817	3,060,291	3,242,526	2,357,455	1,250,653	1,106,802
1983	9,341,058	7,030,386	3,037,065	3,993,321	2,310,672	1,123,804	1,186,868
1984	9,600,383	7,010,890	3,491,783	3,519,107	2,589,493	1,195,030	1,394,463
1985	9,334,245	6,274,841	2,870,024	3,404,817	3,059,404	1,706,831	1,352,573
1986	9,604,636	6,710,465	2,905,324	3,805,141	2,894,170	1,597,629	1,296,541
1987	7,922,097	5,102,041	2,443,368	2,658,673	2,820,056	1,774,154	1,045,902
1988	8,524,108	5,636,184	2,757,526	2,878,658	2,887,925	1,784,043	1,103,881
1989	9,003,794	6,097,899	3,144,204	2,953,695	2,905,895	1,782,533	1,123,362
1990	9,627,333	6,635,580	3,416,151	3,219,429	2,991,754	1,830,943	1,160,810
1991	9,007,065	6,335,941	3,335,459	3,000,483	2,671,123	1,647,379	1,023,744
1992	9,209,902	6,604,920	3,599,991	3,004,929	2,604,982	1,533,474	1,071,508
1993	9,498,291	7,000,797	3,990,808	3,009,989	2,497,495	1,651,985	845,510
1994	10,471,471	7,161,784	4,280,936	2,880,847	3,309,687	2,247,985	1,061,703
1995	9,853,142	7,250,022	4,081,690	3,168,332	2,603,120	1,440,419	1,162,701
1996	9,346,488	7,160,117	4,077,502	3,082,615	2,186,371	1,168,089	1,018,282
1997	10,750,584	7,926,738	4,431,235	3,495,503	2,823,846	1,776,675	1,047,171
1998	10,796,796	7,969,584	4,425,181	3,544,402	2,827,213	1,512,682	1,314,530
1999	9,506,432	6,315,262	3,513,073	2,802,190	3,191,170	1,575,443	1,615,726
2000	9,444,798	6,571,347	3,365,588	3,205,759	2,873,451	1,300,670	1,572,781
2001	9,258,949	6,175,633	3,222,350	2,953,283	3,083,316	1,430,701	1,652,615
2002	8,713,685	5,756,369	2,761,900	2,994,468	2,957,316	1,482,127	1,475,189
2003	9,154,559	6,763,520	3,202,959	3,560,561	2,391,039	1,280,951	1,110,088
2004	10,136,922	7,424,930	3,537,265	3,887,666	2,711,991	1,397,671	1,314,321
2005	11,044,885	7,255,328	3,471,660	3,783,668	3,789,557	1,991,152	1,798,405
2006	10,717,039	6,852,011	3,295,258	3,556,753	3,865,028	1,941,179	1,923,849

Table A.17c—Trends in pulpwood production by species group, Virginia, 1953 to 2006

Year	Total production	Roundwood			Residues		
		Total	Softwood	Hardwood	Total	Softwood	Hardwood
				thousand cubic feet			
1953	86,214	85,847	69,251	16,596	367	128	238
1954	85,802	85,211	69,253	15,957	591	396	195
1955	97,065	95,297	76,251	19,045	1,768	1,207	562
1956	112,216	110,617	85,305	25,312	1,599	1,339	260
1957	102,352	96,377	72,372	24,005	5,975	5,778	197
1958	98,202	93,890	65,777	28,113	4,312	3,990	322
1959	116,816	111,745	83,201	28,544	5,071	4,397	674
1960	123,752	116,677	85,611	31,065	7,076	6,256	819
1961	123,531	113,257	79,731	33,526	10,274	9,151	1,123
1962	127,605	115,064	77,686	37,378	12,541	9,842	2,699
1963	134,038	120,868	82,776	38,091	13,171	9,838	3,333
1964	143,549	128,657	85,332	43,325	14,892	10,810	4,082
1965	163,621	143,820	93,840	49,980	19,801	13,511	6,291
1966	162,530	138,139	87,928	50,210	24,391	14,709	9,682
1967	165,539	134,162	84,192	49,970	31,377	17,875	13,502
1968	166,315	122,392	72,160	50,232	43,923	29,613	14,310
1969	169,966	130,524	68,152	62,371	39,443	26,465	12,978
1970	179,637	142,744	75,431	67,313	36,893	22,059	14,834
1971	179,309	139,158	71,129	68,028	40,151	23,770	16,382
1972	172,418	136,116	67,374	68,742	36,302	19,824	16,478
1973	197,282	144,572	68,753	75,818	52,710	29,546	23,164
1974	202,030	139,373	71,243	68,129	62,657	31,323	31,334
1975	178,001	116,148	58,752	57,395	61,853	37,392	24,462
1976	212,039	148,939	73,875	75,064	63,100	37,485	25,615
1977	199,802	131,979	63,055	68,924	67,823	41,240	26,583
1978	199,947	138,820	67,936	70,884	61,127	30,897	30,230
1979	201,420	128,333	68,111	60,222	73,087	34,129	38,958
1980	233,508	164,742	84,996	79,746	68,766	36,450	32,316
1981	245,937	181,470	83,232	98,238	64,467	35,796	28,671
1982	253,139	184,371	90,468	93,903	68,769	36,465	32,304
1983	272,834	205,427	89,781	115,646	67,407	32,766	34,640
1984	287,269	211,726	102,555	109,171	75,543	34,843	40,699
1985	272,139	182,896	84,294	98,603	89,242	49,766	39,477
1986	280,501	195,526	85,330	110,196	84,975	48,038	36,936
1987	233,714	150,572	74,810	75,762	83,142	53,346	29,796
1988	251,551	166,460	84,429	82,031	85,091	53,643	31,448
1989	263,434	177,833	94,278	83,555	85,601	53,598	32,003
1990	281,628	193,504	102,432	91,072	88,123	55,054	33,070
1991	263,590	184,891	100,013	84,879	78,699	49,534	29,165
1992	262,465	189,411	105,052	84,359	73,054	43,305	29,750
1993	271,084	200,958	116,457	84,501	70,126	46,652	23,475
1994	298,758	205,798	124,923	80,876	92,960	63,482	29,477
1995	274,323	201,365	113,741	87,624	72,958	40,677	32,281
1996	260,136	198,878	113,624	85,253	61,258	32,986	28,272
1997	299,400	220,154	123,481	96,672	79,247	50,173	29,074
1998	300,552	221,337	123,313	98,025	79,215	42,718	36,497
1999	264,549	175,200	97,664	77,536	89,349	44,490	44,859
2000	262,664	182,267	93,564	88,703	80,397	36,730	43,667
2001	256,732	170,446	89,200	81,246	86,286	40,403	45,883
2002	239,908	158,833	76,454	82,379	81,075	40,725	40,350
2003	252,023	186,462	89,198	97,264	65,561	35,197	30,364
2004	279,061	204,707	98,508	106,200	74,354	38,404	35,950
2005	303,603	199,701	96,316	103,385	103,902	54,711	49,191
2006	294,567	188,607	91,422	97,185	105,960	53,338	52,622

www.ingramcontent.com/pod-product-compliance
Lightning Source LLC
Chambersburg PA
CBHW080552290526
45790CB00006B/2633